Travel Abroad:

Frulovisi's *Peregrinatio*

Medieval and Renaissance Texts and Studies

Volume 2 5 1

Neo-Latin Texts and Translations
Volume 2

TRAVEL ABROAD:

Frulovisi's *Peregrinatio*

Translated and with an Introduction

by

Grady Smith

Arizona Center for Medieval and Renaissance Studies
Tempe, Arizona
2003

*Generous grants from George Mason University and
Pegasus Limited for the Promotion of Neo-Latin Studies
have assisted with meeting the publication costs of this volume.*

Dust jacket image: First page of *Peregrinatio.* Cambridge University Library, St John's College, MS. C. 10, fol. 97r. Reproduced by permission of the Masters and Fellows of St John's College, Cambridge.

Library of Congress Cataloging-in-Publication Data

Foro-Juliensis, Titus Livius de.
  [Peregrinatio. English & Latin]
  Travel abroad : Frulovisi's Peregrinatio / translated and with an introduction by
  Grady Smith.
    p. cm. — (Medieval & Renaissance Texts & Studies ; v. 251. Neo-Latin texts
  and translations ; v. 2)
  Text in Latin with English translation on opposite pages.
  Includes bibliographical references and index.
  ISBN 0-86698-294-9 (acid-free paper)
    I. Crete (Greece) — Drama. 2. Rhodes (Greece : Island) — Drama. 3. Latin
  drama (Comedy) — Translations into English. I. Smith, Grady, 1937– II. Title.
  III. Medieval & Renaissance Texts & Studies (Series) ; v. 251. IV. Medieval &
  Renaissance Texts & Studies (Series). Neo-Latin texts and translations ; 2.

PA8520.F9P47 2003
872'.04—dc21   2003040345

CONTENTS

ACKNOWLEDGMENTS

I acknowledge with thanks the assistance of Joan Carr with the Greek passages in *Peregrinatio*. Greg Staley likewise assisted with the Greek, and in addition provided insight, wisdom and friendship. Judy Hallett and the Classics Department of the University of Maryland proved a model of collegiality. Both Jeff Chamberlain and Martin Winkler of George Mason University have supported this project in myriad ways, direct and indirect. I am deeply indebted to Leslie S. B. MacCoull for sifting the entire manuscript with the utmost care, and for her observations and recommendations. And it is a pleasure to thank Robert Coogan for his guidance and support in bringing this work to light as a dissertation.

Finally, I gratefully acknowledge a grant from George Mason University that assisted in the publication of this volume.

INTRODUCTION

From one point of view, Titus Livius Frulovisi was his own worst enemy. Because of his running feuds with rival teachers and some churchmen, he was forced to shut down his Latin school in Venice and become an itinerant humanist. Humphrey, Duke of Gloucester hired him as his poet and orator, but let him go when it became clear he was not as skilled in Greek as the Duke had been led to believe. And he was summarily dismissed by an old schoolmate who had given him a job as a papal subcollector in England — Frulovisi had gotten into an argument with a local priest and been arrested.

But on the other hand, between his first comedy in 1432 and his life of Henry V in 1438, Frulovisi produced a body of work that was studded with significant humanist writings.[1] He admired Plautus and Terence, and in imitation he

---

[1] Frulovisi's extant works and significant scholarship on them are: The comedies: *Corallaria, Claudi Duo,* and *Emporia,* written between September 1432 and August 1433; *Symmachus,* between September 1433 and August 1434; *Oratoria,* between November 1434 and August 1435; *Peregrinatio,* 1437; and *Eugenius,* 1437–38. The plays survive in a single copy at the library of St. John's College, Cambridge, MS. 60, a microfilm of which is held by the Library of Congress. They are printed in *Opera Hactenus Inedita T. Livii Frulovisiis de Ferraria,* ed. C. W. Previté-Orton (Cambridge: Cambridge University Press, 1932). For plot summaries see Previté-Orton's introduction. For dating of the plays, see idem, "The Earlier Career of Titus Livius de Frulovisiis," *English Historical Review* 30 (1915): 75. For the place of Frulovisi's comedies in the scheme of early Italian humanist drama see Giorgio Padoan, "La commedia rinascimentale a Venezia: dalla sperimentazione umanistica alla commedia 'regolare'," in *Dal primo Quattrocento al concilio di Trento,* ed. Girolamo Arnaldi and Manlio Pastore Stocchi (Vicenza: Neri Pozzo Editore, 1981), 3.3: 377–84; and Antonio Stäuble, *La commedia umanistica del Quattrocento* (Firenze: Nella Sede Dell'Istituto Palazzo Strozzi, 1968), 51–65. For a brief view of the influence of Plautus, Terence, and other classical writers in the comedies, see Walther Ludwig, "Titus Livius de' Frulovisi — ein humanistischer Dramatiker der Renaissance," *Humanistica Lovaniensia* 22 (1973): 39–76. For insight into Frulovisi's Latin vocabulary, morphology, and syntax in the comedies, see Outi Merisalo, "Remarks on the Latin of Tito Livio Frulovisi," in *Acta Conventus Neo-Latini Hafniensis,* gen. ed. Rhoda Schnur, MRTS 120 (Binghamton, NY: Medieval and Renaissance Texts and Studies, 1994), 665–68.

The *De Republica* (1435) survives in manuscript at the Biblioteca Municipale in Reggio Emilia (MS. Coll. Turri F. 92), and in Seville's Biblioteca Capitular y Columbina (MS. 7.2.23). Like the plays, it is printed in *Opera.* For a detailed analysis of its Latinity and classical antecedents see Angela Maria Negri Rosio, "Contributi por lo studio del *De re publica* di Tito Livio dei Frulovisi," *Rivista semestrale della biblioteca A. Panizzi,* 1.2 (1977): 129–57; 2.3 (1978): 117–51. Forthcoming from Four Courts Press, Dublin is a translation by Barry Collett with Tor Hanson of the Reggio Emilia MS.

The surviving manuscripts of Frulovisi's history, the *Vita Henrici Quinti* (1438), include two copies contemporary to the author, Corpus Christi College, Cambridge MS. 285, and Arundel MS. 12 at the

wrote the oldest surviving neo-Latin comedies actually performed. His *De Republica* is the first description of a Renaissance state, preceding Machiavelli's *The Prince* by a full century. And his *Vita Henrici Quinti* is the first biography of Henry V, and one of a handful of critical references Holinshed used when he wrote about the

College of Arms. A slightly later, inferior copy, MS. Cotton Claudius E. iii, is at the British Library. Thomas Hearne edited and published the *Vita* (Oxford, 1716) using the Cotton MS., but footnoting the variants in the superior Cambridge MS. 285. Helen Louise St. John, "The *Vita Henrici Quinti* of Tito Livio Frulovisi" (Master's thesis, University of Notre Dame, 1974), provides the Latin text and an English translation. Her Ph.D. dissertation, "A Critical Edition of the *Vita Henrici Quinti* of Tito Livio Frulovisi" (University of Toronto, 1982), satisfies a significant scholarly need in Frulovisi studies. For analysis of the *Vita* see eadem, "A Critical Edition"; Charles L. Kingsford, "The Early Biographies of Henry V," *English Historical Review* 25 (1910): 58–92; and Antonia Gransden, *Historical Writing in England: vol. 2, c.1307 to the Early Sixteenth Century* (Ithaca: Cornell University Press, 1985), 210–12. Also see Constance Blackwell, "Humanism and Politics in English Royal Biography: the Use of Cicero, Plutarch and Sallust in the *Vita Henrici Quinti* (1438) by Titus Livius de Frulovisi . . . ," in *Acta Conventus Neo-Latini Sanctandreani*, ed. I. D. McFarlane, MRTS 38 (Binghamton, NY: Medieval and Renaissance Texts and Studies, 1986), 431–35. Professor Outi Merisalo of the University of Jyväskylä, Finland is now preparing a critical edition of the *Vita*.

Of Frulovisi's Latin poetry, the *Panegyricos Humfroidos* (1436–37) survives uniquely, in the Biblioteca Capitular y Columbina MS. 7.2.23. The existence of the MS. was not generally known when Previté-Orton published the *Opera*, and the poem has never been printed. For a criticism, see Roberto Weiss, "Humphrey, Duke of Gloucester and Tito Livio Frulovisi," in *Fritz Saxl, 1890–1948: A Volume of Memorial Essays from his Friends in England*, ed. D. J. Gordon (London: Thomas Nelson and Sons, 1957), 221–27. The *Encomium Episcopi Bathoniensis* (1438) survives in a single copy immediately following the *Vita* in MS. Cotton Claudius E. iii. It is also printed in the *Opera*, the introduction of which contains an evaluation.

Some significant correspondence to and from Frulovisi appears in Remigio Sabbadini, "Tito Livio Frulovisio, umanista del secolo XV," *Giornale storico della letteratura italiana* 103 (1934): 55–81: Bruni to Frulovisi concerning a translation of Aristotle's *Politics* commissioned by Humphrey; two letters of Montanus about Frulovisi's employment as a papal subcollector; and Frulovisi's request to Decembrio for copies of medical works, and Decembrio's reply. In addition, Frulovisi to Decembrio and Decembrio's reply are also reproduced by Mario Borsa, "Pier Candido Decembri e l'umanesimo in Lombardia," *Archivio storico lombardo*, ser. 2, 20 (1893): 428–29. Bruni's letter also appears in *Leonardi Bruni Aretini Epistolarum Libri VIII ad Fidem Codd. Mss. Suppleti*, ed. Lorenzo Mehus (Florence: ex typographia Bernardi Paperini, 1741), 2: 98–99.

John Koelhoff the Elder printed *De Orthographia* at Cologne in 1480, erroneously ascribing authorship to Frulovisi. Major parts of two separate works make up this book, one with the same title by Gasparino Barzizza, the other the *Ars Diphthongandi* of Guarino. On the issue of authorship, see M. Lehnerdt, "Review," in *Gnomon* 10 (1934): 158–59.

In her paper on the *De Republica* ("Contributi," 1, 129 n. 2), Angela Maria Negri Rosio provides a thorough Frulovisi bibliography, beginning at the end of the seventeenth century. Since her paper is difficult of access, I provide her citations to the end of the nineteenth century: G. I. Vossius, *De Historicis Latinis Liber III*, pars altera (Amsterdam, 1699), 225; T. Rymer, *Foedera* (London, 1704–1735), 10: 661–62; *Acta Eruditorum Mensis Aprilis a. MDCCXVII* (Leipzig, 1717), 167–68; *Giornale dei letterati d'Italia* 28 (Venice, 1717): 400; C. Oudinus, *Commentarius de Scriptoribus Ecclesiasticis* (Leipzig, 1722); 3: col. 2309; G. Degli Agostini, *Historia degli scrittori viniziani* (Venice, 1752), 1: 66; J. A. Fabricius, *Bibliotheca Latina Mediae et Infimae Aetatis* (Padua, 1754), 4: 278, 6: 274; G. Tiraboschi, *Storia della letteratura italiana*, 16 (Milan, 1828), 213–14; H. Anstey, *Monimenta Academica* (London, 1868) 2: 769; G. Voigt, *Il rinascimento dell'antichità classica ovvero il primo secolo dell'umanesimo*, trad. di D. Valbusa, vol. 2 (Florence, 1890), 248 e vol. 3, Giunte & correzioni & indici a cura di G. Zippel (Florence, 1897), 55; M. Borsa, "Pier Candido Decembri e l'umanesimo in Lombardia," *Archivio storico lombardo*, ser. 2, 20 (1893): 63, 428–29.

king in his *Chronicles* — a work which was in turn one of Shakespeare's major historical sources.

Looking at these professional triumphs cheek by jowl with his personal defeats suggests inevitable questions. Who exactly was this Frulovisi? What was his training? How did humanism, gathering momentum in early quattrocento Italy, shape his ambitions and his work? What flaws of character brought him down? And what legacy of his emerges from an age in which an entrenched medieval Christian outlook fought stubbornly against an intellectual movement that idealized pagan wisdom and thought?

LIFE AND WORK

Quite a bit is known about Frulovisi, both from records of the period and from his own writings. His father moved the family to Venice not long after his son's birth in Ferrara. There is some question whether Domenico named his son Titus Livius, after the Roman historian Livy, or if the young man adopted it himself when he later decided to pursue a humanist career. Certainly it would have been difficult to find a priest willing to baptize an infant with the name of a pre-Christian pagan.

In any case, the boy was raised and educated in the capital city at a time when the Venetian Republic was expanding its hegemony on the mainland, as well as its financial dealings and cultural horizons through both land and seaborne exchange. The young Frulovisi learned his Latin and some Greek under Guarino da Verona, the preeminent humanist teacher in Italy at the time. Since Guarino was resident in Venice from 1414 to 1419, Frulovisi was likely born around 1400 or so.[2]

After working for a time as a notary public, he decided to teach and set up a boys' academy in the parish of Santo Basso about 1429.[3] Three years later he wrote *Corallaria*, the first of five Latin comedies he would produce at his school on festival days. He would later round out his playwriting with two more Latin comedies written in England.

---

[2] Guarino taught in several cities in the early part of his career: Florence (1410–1414), Venice (1414–1419), his native Verona (1419–1429), and finally Ferrara, where he died in 1460. See Remigio Sabbadini, *Vita di Guarino Veronese* (Genova: Sordomuti, 1891; repr. Turin: Bottega D'Erasmo, 1964), 96 (page citations are to the reprint edition).

[3] Contemporary references to Frulovisi are infrequent outside of his own writings and exchanges of correspondence. In one such, 12 April 1429, he is listed ("Titus Livius Perlovisiis") in his notarial function as a witness, and is further identified as the son of Domenico and *rector scholarum* in the parish of Santo Basso. See Enrico Bertanza and Giuseppe Dalla Santa, *Documenti per la storia della cultura in Venezia*, vol. I, *Maestri, scuole, e scolari in Venezia fina al 1500* (Venezia: a Spese della Società, 1907), I: 315.

Corallaria created an immediate controversy. In its prologue Frulovisi claimed that the work was original: "We don't bring old plays. ... Old plays are trite. ... What's new delights, what's new pleases, what's old brings on senility" [non adducimus veteres fabulas. ... veteres sunt ita tritae. ... nova delectant, nova placent, vetera senium inducunt] (6).[4] Notwithstanding, he was accused of plagiarism by Jacopo Langosco, a sometime professor at the University of Padua and a ducal secretary in the Venetian government. Langosco charged that *Corallaria* was cribbed from an unnamed comedy of his own that has not survived.[5]

In the tradition of Terence, Frulovisi used the prologue of his next play, *Claudi Duo*, to rebut Langosco and his allies with frank polemics. In defending himself he abandoned his earlier claim of originality. He borrowed freely from Plautus, he said, just as the Roman comic writers helped themselves to the works of earlier Greek playwrights. In fact, Frulovisi lifted portions of his rebuttal straight from Terentian prologues. Here is Terence, engaging a rival playwright in *Eunuchus*:

exclamat furem, non poetam fabulam dedisse (ll. 23–24)[6]

[He screams that the author is a thief, and not the playwright]

In *Andria* Terence addresses a more numerous opposition:

qui quom hunc accusant, Naevium Plautum Ennium accusant, quos hic noster auctores habet (ll. 18–19).

[When they accuse this author, they accuse Naevius, Plautus and Ennius, who in our opinion are the authors.]

And here is Frulovisi:

Hunc Langusci dedisse fabulam, non suam: furem appellant. ... Qui cum Livium accusant, et Plautum accusant, quem hic noster autorem habet. (35)

---

[4] Page numbers in parentheses refer to Previté-Orton, *Opera*.

[5] Frulovisi details the charge and defends himself against it in the prologue to his second play, *Claudi Duo*. See Previté-Orton, *Opera*, 35–36. Margaret L. King, *Venetian Humanism in an Age of Patrician Dominance* (Princeton: Princeton University Press, 1964) provides information on the ducal secretary's position at 294, and on Langosco himself at 386–87.

[6] All Latin texts of Plautus and Terence come from the Loeb Classical Library, published by Harvard University Press. The translations, however, are mine.

[They charge this teacher with having given Langosco's play instead of his own: they call him a thief. ... But when they accuse Livius [i.e., Frulovisi], they also accuse Plautus, who in our opinion is the author.]

But Frulovisi's opponents didn't stop at simply making charges. As he set about producing *Claudi Duo,* he found himself deprived of the professional actors and costumes he used in the earlier *Corallaria,* and had to rely on the help of students and friends. Moreover, his opposition had learned before the performance of *Claudi Duo* that this second play of Frulovisi's, as did some of his Roman models, used pagan deities as characters, and he was reported to church authorities:

Nunc nova dedere: deis quod uti non liceat comoedis. ... Hunc accusant nostro antistiti superstitionis novae. ... Veretur hic pontifices. ... Non orabit Iovem coelesti pompa. (35–36)

[Now you give new false charges: it is not permitted to use pagan deities in comedies. ... They accuse this teacher of *nova superstitio* before the bishop. ... This man respects the hierarchy. ... He will not pray to Jove in the pomp of his heaven.]

This denunciation was not merely minor harassment by his antagonists. Significant elements within the church, dominated by medieval scholasticism, were deeply concerned because the humanists, in their reach back across time, were becoming morally situated in an age before Christ redeemed man. They were greatly troubled by the movement's admiration of pre-Christian pagan wisdom and virtues, and referred to it as the *nova superstitio* — a term which, as has been seen, Frulovisi repeated in his prologue to *Claudi Duo.* These elements insisted on the role of grace in the dynamic of man's virtuous living:

It was this problem of pagan virtue that made it so difficult for some men to accept all the implications of humanism: a return to the world of the Greeks and the Romans was inevitably a return to a world before Christ, and that this should be thought desirable was repugnant to many.[7]

But his enemies' attempt to excite the displeasure of the church was a potent strategy, because the state used the ecclesiastical apparatus as a means of govern-

---

[7] Fred J. Levy, *Tudor Historical Thought* (San Marino, CA: The Huntington Library, 1967), 36.

ance. It even reserved the right to name all bishops within its realm.[8] Frulovisi, in effect, had been brought to the attention of the authorities.

Apparently the enlistment rate rose among Frulovisi's opponents after *Claudi Duo*. A group of rival schoolmasters jointly wrote and produced a play called *Magistrea*, evidently intended as an affront to Frulovisi. Like Langosco's play, the *Magistrea* has been lost, and in fact its existence is known only because Frulovisi mentioned it in the prologue of his third comedy, *Emporia*, to pay it the insult of scant heed. But it must have rankled because he brought it up again in the prologue of his last Venetian comedy, the *Oratoria*.

In *Symmachus*, his fourth comedy, Frulovisi continued to counterattack, although against a generalized "they":

> Haec ubi nova data est, statim comperiunt quod dicant male. ... Ignavii vix aliorum qui dicta sentiant detrectatione sua magnos se credunt viros factos! (107–8)

> [As soon as this new play is presented, they see it at once so that they might criticize it. ... The ignorant, who scarcely grasp what others say, believe they make themselves great men by their detractions!]

The prologue of his fifth comedy, the *Oratoria*, contained no vague "they." Here he returned to polemics with specificity and intensity, going so far as to name one of his primary antagonists from the stage. His particular target was a Dominican, one Fra Leone, about whose life only Frulovisi's intense dislike is known. The playwright began his attack in the prologue through wordplay:

> Iam scholastici vincunt. ... Nos impugnat leo. ... Leo in altis blaterat tronis. Sancti qui sunt, prophanos poetas nominat. ... Mulierculae et leo bestia pro scholasticis hominem impugnant. (154)

> [Now the scholastics conquer. ... A lion attacks us. ... A lion roars among the lofty thrones. They who are sacred in their calling he describes as irreligious poets. ... Foolish women and the lion-beast attack the man on behalf of the scholastics.]

He extended his attack in the *Oratoria* by using Fra Leone as a character, Friar Leocyon ("lion-dog"). In a subplot this Dominican attempts to seduce the beau-

---

[8] King, *Venetian Humanism*, 219.

tiful young Hagna when she comes to him in the confessional, and she runs away amidst uproar. Later he disguises himself as a Roman noble and loudly announces his love outside her window. The bishop orders his arrest but at the end of the play he breaks out of prison and escapes. The real Fra Leone could not have been much pleased. Later Frulovisi would add an explanatory gloss to the manuscript of the work's fair copy:

> Leocyon vero nomen fratris cuiusdam qui praedicaverat me et omnes poetas esse excom‹m›unicatos: quamvis solum vocaretur leo. Sed ad maius decus additur κύων quod est canis ad demonstrandum quod dupliciter erat bestia. (158)

> [Leocyon is in fact the name of a certain friar who had declared me and all poets to be excommunicated: although his name is just "Leo." But as a greater honor, -cyon, which means dog, is added to show that he was also a jackal, a beast twice over.]

A slashing attack against Fra Leone, no question — followed in the prologue of the *Oratoria* by Frulovisi's complete capitulation. He has decided to resign the field:

> Quinta fuerit *Oratoria*, quam vobis dabit, et ultima. Heu, heu, ultima. Nos deo bestiae privant, virtute tanta. Flete, iuvenes, flete de ignavis crabronibus, leone, et bestiis impugnari bonos. (154)

> [*Oratoria* is the fifth comedy he will present to you, and the last. Alas, yes, the last. The beasts deprive us of God,[9] of so much virtue. Weep, young students, weep at the contemptible hornets, the lion, and the beasts assaulting good men.]

This surrender of Frulovisi's involved not only abandoning the writing of comedies, but also forsaking teaching. He had produced the *Oratoria* some time between November 1434 and August 1435. After the performance he resigned his position at Santo Basso, and probably undertook an Italian journey during which he worked on his *De Republica*. He writes that he completed this work at Venice in 1435.[10]

---

[9] Perhaps a reference to Fra Leone's assertion that he should be excommunicated?

[10] "Autor composuit Venetiis in milesimo quadringentesimo trigesimo quinto tempore illustrissimi principis domini Francisci Foscari." Paul Oskar Kristeller quotes this sentence from the end of the MS.,

The first representation of a Renaissance state, the *De Republica* is unequivocally a milestone. For matter, Frulovisi mined the letters of Petrarch and Salutati, Cicero's *De Officiis* and *De Inventione*, the histories of Livy and Justin, Aristotle's *Politics*, and other Greek, Roman, and medieval authors.[11]

A comparison of Frulovisi and Cicero in several passages dealing with aspects of justice gives an idea of the former's knowledge of the latter and of their correspondence in parts of the *De Republica*:

Frulovisi	Cicero
Iusticia in anima est habitus quidam ad hominum utilitatem conservatus dignitatemque suam cuique tribuens. (357)	Iustitia est habitus animi communi utilitate conservata suam cuique tribuens dignitatem. (*inv.* 2, 160)
... alteram ne cui quis noceat nisi lacessitus iniuria, et alteram ut communibus pro communibus utatur et privatis ut suis. (373)	Sed justitiae primum munus est, ut ne cui quis noceat nisi lacessitus iniuria, deinde ut communibus pro communibus utatur, privatis ut suis. (*inv.* I, 20)

held by the Biblioteca Capitular y Columbina, in *Iter Italicum: Accedunt Alia Itinera*, vol. 4 (London and New York: The Warburg Institute, E. J. Brill, 1989), 624. While a dated excipit is not always trustworthy, I believe early 1435 is probably the date of the work's completion. Frulovisi taught continuously at least until his last Venetian play *Oratoria* was produced some time between November 1434 and August 1435 (Previté-Orton, "The Earlier Career," 75). The performance of this comedy thus marks the beginning of the period during which Frulovisi's journey to Naples and the subsequent writing of the *De Republica* must have occurred. An earlier starting date while teaching is unlikely since the school year at this time was continuous. Although the year included literally scores of holidays, Frulovisi could not have made his trip to Naples in the limited time available. Neither Easter, with its break of several days, nor even *carnevale* with its seven- or eight-day hiatus, would have been long enough for the journey. See Paul F. Grendler, *Schooling in Renaissance Italy* (Baltimore: Johns Hopkins University Press, 1989), 34. By contrast, the terminus ad quem for the journey and subsequent writing of the *De Republica* occurs with the death of Joanna II of Naples on 2 February 1435, a major event conspicuous by its absence in Frulovisi's work. Moreover Louis III of Anjou, who had been investing Naples since 1433 to enforce his claim to its throne, died in November 1434. The cessation of hostilities following Louis's death would have facilitated Frulovisi's journey. Thus he likely made his way to Naples no earlier than November 1434 and began work on the MS. after his return. On the basis of these facts I would agree with the excipit and assign the final completion of the *De Republica* to some time in January 1435. I thank Professor Barry Collett of the University of Melbourne for calling to my attention Joanna's death and its implications for the dating of the *De Republica*.

[11] Negri Rosio, "Contributi," 2, 124–44, gives a detailed analysis of the correspondences between Frulovisi and a number of classical authors.

Et cum iniusticiae partes duae quoque
sint: inferri iniuriam alteri, quod nusquam rex committat, et ab aliis quum
potest si non propulsat. (373)

Sed iniustitiae genera duo sunt, unum
eorum, qui inferunt, alterum eorum,
qui ab iis quibus infertur, si possunt,
non propulsant iniuriam. (*inv.* I, 23)

Though Frulovisi made free use of Cicero, he was at pains, having been
bloodied in polemics with the scholastics, to recast Ciceronian references to pagan
deities into a doctrinally acceptable format. Angela Maria Negri Rosio points
out,[12] for example, that where Cicero in defining religion refers to *superioris cuiusdam
naturae quam divinam vocant* and *deorum* (*inv.* 2, 161; 2, 66), Frulovisi carefully shades
his borrowings toward Christian orthodoxy: *Religio Dei veri cultus est* (357).

For form, playwright Frulovisi chose the dialogue. This genre reached its original maturity in fifth-century B.C. Greece. Cicero refined it by changing the setting
from historical to contemporary, examining philosophical principles and generaliz-
ations in light of empirical experience within the Roman civic process, and fully
presenting the arguments on both sides of an issue. Augustine modified the medieval dialogue by turning it into an introspective colloquy between aspects of the
self. This state of affairs more or less obtained until the threshold of the quattrocento when in 1401 Leonardo Bruni wrote his *Dialogi ad Petrum Histrum*, which re-
connected the form to its classical antecedents. Bruni's work began to stimulate a
resurgence of interest in the form and a return to its use.

Twenty years after Bruni's *Dialogi*, a discovery intensified this interest and use.
For the humanists, Cicero was preeminent among the ancients because of the
acuity of his thought and the grace of his Latin, and when in 1421 Bishop Gerar-
do Landriani found a complete manuscript of Cicero's principal works on rhetoric, they were electrified. Among other works, some previously known only in
fragments or not at all, it contained the entire text of the *De Oratore*,[13] Cicero's
greatest dialogue,[14] known earlier only through imperfect and mutilated manuscripts. With Cicero as classical paradigm and Bruni as contemporary exemplar,

---

[12] Negri Rosio, "Contributi," 2, 131 n. 136.

[13] Landriani, bishop of Lodi, made his discovery while searching for some ancient charters pertain-
ing to the status of his diocese. He opened a long-neglected trunk and found a complete manuscript of
the principal works of Cicero on rhetoric. The *De Oratore* and the *Orator* had hitherto been known only
through imperfect and mutilated manuscripts; the *Brutus* was absolutely new. See John Sandys, *A History
of Classical Scholarship* (New York: Hafner Publishing Co., 1958), 2: 31, and Charles S. Baldwin, *Renaissance
Literary Theory and Practice* (New York: Columbia University Press, 1939), 43–45. *Texts and Transmission:
A Survey of the Latin Classics*, ed. Leighton D. Reynolds (Oxford: Clarendon Press, 1983), 102–9, details
the preservation and dissemination of the text of *De Oratore*.

[14] David Marsh, *The Quattrocento Dialogue* (Cambridge and London: Harvard University Press, 1980),
3.

humanists began gravitating to the dialogue with avidity, using it for significant documents and issues, and transforming it into one of the signature genres of the humanist movement. Thus the 1435 *De Republica* lies squarely in the midst of the dialogue's resurgence in its Ciceronian mode, and constitutes an appropriate setting for this first examination of the Renaissance state.[15]

So Frulovisi selected the dialogue form probably because of its currency as well as because it played to the strengths of his own literary experience, although his stated rationale only addresses the latter reason:

> Volui in hunc libellum ... illorum sententias litteris mandasse, bonos principes introducens et me loquentem, cum ut morem servarem qui habitus est a me in comoediis, tum ne 'inquam' et 'inquit' crebra positio fastidium ullum auribus tuis movere posset. (296)

> [I wished in this book ... to commit their opinions to writing, bringing in the good princes and myself speaking, so that while I preserve the usage which I have had in the comedies, at the same time I avoid the crowding together of 'I say' and 'he says' lest it could stir any repugnance in your ears.]

With respect to the structure of the work, just as Cicero divided the *Tusculanae Disputationes* into five books with the conversations presented as if occurring over five days, so Frulovisi organized the *De Republica* into three books and three days. The prologue describes how, during the course of a journey through Italy, he had a series of conversations at Naples with the Count of Buccino (d. after 1460) and Chancellor Ottino Caracciolo (d. c. 1443) which ultimately resulted in the *De Republica*.

The dedication of the work to Leonello d'Este, heir to the throne of Ferrara, tends to confirm that Frulovisi hoped for employment in the city of his birth as the prince's poet and orator. Frulovisi's old teacher Guarino was Leonello's tutor until the prince's 1435 wedding, and perhaps Frulovisi used his good offices to gain access to the prince, with the *De Republica* serving as a writing sample. But no offer of employment was made, surely in part because of the playwright's quarrels in Venice.

---

[15] Virginia Cox, *The Renaissance Dialogue*, Cambridge Studies in Renaissance Literature and Culture 2 (Cambridge: Cambridge University Press, 1992), 23–24, 61–63. Although the primary focus of this work is on the dialogue from the beginning of the sixteenth century, it provides some pertinent observations on the use of the genre in the quattrocento as well.

When things seemed darkest for Frulovisi, he received an offer from England to become the poet and orator of Humphrey, Duke of Gloucester. Frulovisi was probably recommended by the papal collector in England, Petrus Montanus[16] — a recommendation the collector would later come to regret. A Venetian, Montanus had studied Greek with Frulovisi under Guarino.[17] Possibly Humphrey interviewed Frulovisi in August 1436 when the Duke was briefly in Flanders.[18] Whether or not the meeting actually took place, in all likelihood Frulovisi made a copy of the *De Republica* available as a sample of his work.[19]

Gloucester had sought the services of an Italian humanist for some time. He wanted someone who could draft his correspondence in the humanist style, produce other works typical of the new learning, and translate Greek classics into Latin for the use of English scholars. Before Frulovisi's arrival he offered the position to Leonardo Aretino, who declined because of age.[20] He eventually replaced Frulovisi with Antonio Beccaria, whose rendering of the writings of Athanasius into Latin was the first instance in that century of a translation from the Greek made in England.[21] So Frulovisi joined Humphrey's household some time after August 1436, and on 7 March 1437 was granted denization.[22]

While he was in England, Frulovisi's literary production continued at a high level of intensity. The *Humfroidos Panegyricos* was circulated almost immediately, in late 1436 or early 1437.[23] This poem, which celebrates Gloucester's deeds from the conference at Arras to his laying waste Flanders after lifting the siege at Calais, acts as one element in a campaign by Gloucester to construct a heroic per-

---

[16] Johannes Haller, *Piero da Monte* (Rome: W. Regensberg, 1941), *82.

[17] In one of his letters to Frulovisi, Montanus, a known student of Guarino's, states "monet me hec litterarum ac studiorum communio quam mecum habes": Sabbadini, "Tito Livio Frulovisio," 76, from Cod. Vat. Lat. 2694, 176r.

[18] Alfredo Sammut, *Unfredo duca di Gloucester e gli umanisti italiani* (Padua: Editrice Antenore, 1980), 18.

[19] A copy of the *De Republica* is listed as Gloucester's in H. H. E. Craster, "Index to Duke Humphrey's Gifts to the Old Library of the University in 1439, 1441, and 1444," *Bodleian Quarterly Record* 1 (1914–1916): 131. On the later missing status of Humphrey's donations, see B. L. Ullman, "Manuscripts of Duke Humphrey of Gloucester," *English Historical Review* 52 (1937): 670.

[20] Aretino responded to Gloucester's invitation on 12 March 1433: "The praises and commendations and proposals set forth in your letter mean so much to me, that I cannot think of anything that could be better or finer. If only the condition of the times or my age [63] permitted, how your kind invitation to come to your country would be fulfilled!" Quoted in Ralph A. Griffiths, *The Reign of King Henry VI* (Berkeley: University of California Press, 1981), 154.

[21] Grady Smith, "Books and the Development of English Humanism," *Fifteenth-Century Studies* 6 (1983): 232 and n. 13. See also James W. Binns, "Latin Translations from the Greek," in idem, *Intellectual Culture in Elizabethan and Jacobean England* (Leeds: Francis Cairns Ltd., 1990), 215–40. Binns comprehensively details the translations into Latin from the Greek made during the Tudor age, when the efforts of Gloucester and others to make Greek part of British cultural life finally came to fruition.

[22] Thomas Rymer, *Foedera* (London: A. & J. Churchhill, 1704–1735), 10: 660–61.

[23] Griffiths, *Henry VI*, 224–25. See also Gransden, *Historical Writing*, 210–11.

sona for himself. That campaign culminated in the very positive reception given him by parliament in January 1437. Frulovisi's sixth play, *Peregrinatio* (1437), was his initial comedic effort in England, followed by his final play, *Eugenius* (1437 or 1437–38). He completed the *Vita Henrici Quinti* (1438) as the end of his service approached, and the *Encomium Episcopi Bathoniensis* (1438 or 1439) was the unfinished draft of an eleventh-hour plea to the chancellor, Bishop John Stafford, for assistance.

Frulovisi apparently never attempted to translate from the Greek, his mastery of the language being too superficial. He perhaps hoped his playwriting would be an acceptable substitute. But Gloucester seems to have been unimpressed, for while all five Venetian comedies were staged, neither of his British plays received a production.

Why was Frulovisi let go by Humphrey after less than three years' service? Professionally, stylistic weaknesses became clear: his Greek proved too shallow and his Latin too colloquially idiomatic — apt for comedy, less so for the biography of a king.[24] Personally, the reasons are more complex. To begin with, he seems unaware of the effect of his writing on his patron. In the prologue to *Peregrinatio*, for example, Frulovisi, seemingly unable to let go of a quarrel, continued to engage his old enemies in Venice and, crowning a rhetorical flourish, he wrote: "Neither by princes nor anyone else will our talent be silenced" [non principibus nec aliis clausa virtus erit nostri] (187). Not a politic utterance in a work first and foremost for the eyes of the Duke of Gloucester, who from September 1435 was heir apparent to the English throne.

Frulovisi seems even less aware of the effects on Humphrey of the theme of divorce he built into the *Eugenius*, a work, he states in the prologue, in which the title character is frankly modeled on Gloucester: "You will see yourself in another as in a mirror" [in alio quasi per speculum te videbis] (224).

But this theme cannot have been welcome to the duke. Humphrey, during the 1420s, married Jacqueline of Hainault in a hasty and ecclesiastically dubious ceremony because he wanted to become the ruler of her lands. He was, after all, the fourth son of a king and unlikely otherwise to achieve a rule of his own. Jacqueline was married, but claimed the union was invalid because of her husband's brutishness. When Rome seemed reluctant to agree with her, the couple secured a decree of nullity from one of the last antipopes of the Great Schism. Moving with Jacqueline to her lands put Gloucester in a better position to achieve his personal goals. Unfortunately, however, it also set him at odds with the Duke of Burgundy,

---

[24] See St. John's evaluation in "A Critical Edition," 16–17.

England's ally in Europe against the French, and it consequently put England's continental policy at risk. In effect, Humphrey subordinated national interests to personal ambition.

At home he was quickly in trouble, and in Hainault he was unable to generate a crucial popularity among the people, particularly the merchant class. Gloucester found a way out of this dangerous impasse when Rome, following the death of Jacqueline's first husband, declared that her marriage had indeed been valid and she and Humphrey would have to repeat their wedding ceremony. Humphrey declined and left Hainault, ostensibly for reinforcements, abandoning Jacqueline to an uncertain future.[25]

Evidently Frulovisi believed that the divorce motif in *Eugenius* would stimulate Humphrey's sense of place and privilege. But surely it also evoked the failure of his quest for a rule of his own, rejection by Rome in refusing to dissolve Jacqueline's first marriage, the reckless endangerment of England's continental policy by his pursuit of personal goals, and his callous abandonment of Jacqueline after his own failures. The effect of *Eugenius* on Gloucester cannot have been the one Frulovisi intended.

Besides this blindness to the effects of his writing on his patron, Frulovisi apparently had money problems. Certainly the subject preoccupied him: in the prologue to *Eugenius* he mentions his patron's generosity in pro forma ways, then dwells at length on the wealth bestowed upon Dante, Virgil, and Seneca by their benefactors. The context presents these examples of extravagant patronage to Humphrey without much subtlety.

Frulovisi also had expensive tastes when books were in question — at least his own books. The unique manuscript of his plays was copied and decorated in the duke's scriptorium by the same artisans who had produced the presentation copy of the *Vita Henrici Quinti*. Whether he had unlimited use of the scriptorium or ought to have provided reimbursement for this personal project is not known. But the decoration of the plays is sumptuous, with rich blues and greens, and a generous use of gold leaf. One critic speculates that the reason this fair copy of the plays remained behind in England is that the book may have been seized for debt.[26] In any case, in his hurried and incomplete poem, the *Encomium Episcopi Bathoniensis*, Frulovisi tells the English chancellor that he is in debt and cannot even

---

[25] Ernest F. Jacob, *The Fifteenth Century, 1399–1485* (Oxford: Clarendon Press, 1961), 225–26; C. Oman, *The History of England from the Accession of Richard II to the Death of Richard III (1377–1485)*, The Political History of England, vol. 4 (Longmans, Green & Co., 1906; repr. New York: Greenwood Press Publishers, 1969), 292, 296; Griffiths, *Henry VI*, 179; Bertram Wolffe, *Henry VI* (London: Eyre Methuen, 1981), 38–39.

[26] Previté-Orton, *Opera*, xviii.

set out for Italy. He asks for a position under the king or help in leaving for home. He describes himself as "a man of undisciplined character always on the brink of disaster" [languida virtus semper ad extremum] (391).

And then there is Frulovisi's unfortunate personal comportment. So obvious in Venice, it also surfaced in England. About the time Humphrey terminates his service, his old classmate Montanus excoriates Frulovisi at length in a letter, accusing him of ingratitude and of bringing Montanus into disrepute by associating their names together. He even charges Frulovisi with selling information, presumably about Humphrey, and then disparages Frulovisi's work as a playwright:

> Aures profecto habes nimium faciles easque libenter prebes quibusdam malivolis aliter quam doctum ac sapientem virum deceat. Horum autem detrahentium commenta et fraudes quibus, ut apud comicum est: solent ex stultis insanos facere.[27]

> [You have exceedingly sharp ears indeed and willingly offer them to certain malicious people in a way that is otherwise than seemly to a wise and learned man. To the wise, however, these slanderous comments and deceits are like what is found in the works of a writer of comedy, because such wise men are accustomed to making foolish people out to be mad.]

After rounding on Frulovisi so fiercely, Montanus begins to exhort him. If Frulovisi wishes to be taken for a wise, learned, and educated man, indeed for a philosopher, why then doesn't he produce works of philosophy? He should read the lives of illustrious men, admiring their deeds and praising their characters. He should always have a book in his hand. But these activities are in vain if they do not result in increased knowledge, goodness, and prudence. Frulovisi should make himself receptive to Montanus's counsel and not let himself be dominated by his emotions. A good and learned man "ought to refrain from every vituperation, from every injury, and have custody not only of his hands but of his eyes and tongue as well" [debet ab omni maledicto, ab omni iniuria abstinere et non solum manus sed et oculos et linguam habere continentem].[28] If Frulovisi is prepared to conform to these exhortations, Montanus is ready to employ him as a subcollector — where, by implication, Montanus can keep his eye on him. Frulovisi accepts.

---

[27] Sabbadini, "Tito Livio Frulovisio," 74–75. The letter bears a July date but lacks a year. Sabbadini assigns it to 1439 based on the full dating of the letters immediately preceding and following it in Cod. Vat. Lat. 2694.

[28] Sabbadini, "Tito Livio Frulovisio," 77.

Twelve months later, with Montanus about to send him to the papal curia on business, Frulovisi wrote his superior from his subcollector's district to tell him he had been arrested on the complaint of a local priest, Johannes Gele. Montanus's terse reply wonders why the priest was so antagonistic, unless Frulovisi dropped all restraints of tongue,

> ... ut soles. Quod cum facis, neque etati neque dignitati parcis magnaque in te etiam potentum odia provocas. ... Nisi linguam tuam compescueris, tandem in foveam cades.[29]

> [... as is your habit. When you do such a thing, you spare neither age nor rank, and provoke against yourself the deep hatreds of the powerful. ... Unless you curb your tongue, sooner or later you will end up in a ditch.]

Then comes the termination. Master John had already been assigned to Frulovisi's old job because of the latter's projected absence in Rome, and when Frulovisi failed his departure time, Montanus sent Vincentius Clemens to the curia in his place. Thus there are no vacancies available for Frulovisi. Montanus's farewell is marked by platitudes and coolness: "*Vale*, and if you act faithfully, you'll keep your spirits up. I'll never be far from you in your difficulties. Again, *vale*" [Vale, et si ex fide egeris, bono animo sis, quoniam ego numquam tuis necessitatibus deero. Iterum vale].[30]

Frulovisi's stay in England, then, began some months before his March 1437 denization. The letters of Montanus show that it moved in a new direction in July 1439 when the papal collector, as has been seen, employed Frulovisi as one of his subcollectors. And he must have left as soon as possible after Montanus dismissed him in the spring of 1440.[31]

His sojourn was thus marked by two successive reverses. After Gloucester let him go for a combination of professional and personal reasons, Montanus in effect fired him for his reckless temper and tongue. Circumstances then forced

---

[29] Sabbadini, "Tito Livio Frulovisio," 79. Sabbadini bases the date of this letter, the spring of 1440, on the dating of its neighbors in Cod. Vat. Lat. 2694.

[30] Sabbadini, "Tito Livio Frulovisio," 79.

[31] Previté-Orton, *Opera*, xv, writing two years before Sabbadini was to print Montanus's letters to Frulovisi, hypothesized a return to Italy at an unspecified time soon after the writing of the *Encomium*. Remigio Sabbadini (1850–1934), in his posthumously published "Tito Livio Frulovisio," 60, ignores the contents of the letters his paper publishes, and without documentation declares the return a fact. Sammut, *Unfredo*, 19, citing Sabbadini, repeats the error, as does Weiss, *Humanism in England*, 40. Haller, *Piero da Monte*, 164 n. 1, remarks that Sabbadini was incorrect in thinking Frulovisi had returned to Venice.

Frulovisi to make major changes in his personal goals. Those changes become clear through a letter, c. 1442, which he wrote from Barcelona to his friend Decembrio, the chancellor of Milan. The letter forwards a copy of the *Vita Henrici Quinti*, which Decembrio later translated into Italian, and requests books. Frulovisi begins thus:

> Sic ratio mearum peregrinationum exigit me quod interdum versipellem faciam.[32] Ego a vobis abiens, ut verum non inficiar, ex principibus nauseans adeo stomachatus sum, ut ipsorum ieiunium aliquantisper sit habendum cum popularibus viventi.[33]

> [The manner of my travels thus requires me now and then to alter my outward image. After leaving you, granted, yes, I wasn't poisoned; still I was nauseated by princes to the point where I churned, so for a fairly long time I've been abstaining from them by living among the people.]

He then mentions rather breezily that while in Toulouse he was declared *inter physicos et artistas doctor*, and is now in Barcelona — although not practicing medicine because the plague makes it too dangerous. He asks Decembrio to have certain medical works copied and sent, and agrees beforehand to pay any expenses: "I won't delay, nor forget myself, nor haggle over your costs" [Ego non tardabo neque me negligentem, neque rei minus cupidum dices].[34] Decembrio responds with a kind, if paternal, letter:

> Bene agis qui tempori pares et te noscis. Principibus enim usque adeo parendum est, quoad meritas virtuti gratias impendunt. Non enim is princeps habendus est, qui in judicando fallitur, in promerendo ac demerendo plus voluptati quam rationi favere solet.[35]

> [You act well when you obey the time and know yourself. For one will obey princes even to the last detail until they parcel out rewards for dedicated service. But that one isn't to be considered a prince who is mistaken in judging, and accustomed in weighing merit and demerit to favor pleasure more than reason.]

---

[32] Plautus, *Amphitryon* 123: "In this way he shifts his shape whenever he wants" [Ita versipellem se facit quando lubet].

[33] Sabbadini, "Tito Livio Frulovisio," 80.

[34] Sabbadini, "Tito Livio Frulovisio," 80.

[35] Sabbadini, "Tito Livio Frulovisio," 81.

He compliments Frulovisi on the *Vita*, and promises to send the requested books. Then, gently disputing the wisdom of altering the outward image that he shows the world (the idiom Frulovisi used, *versipellem facere*, connotes slyness or craftiness), he proposes that the quality of one's character is best revealed in the worthiness of one's actions:

> Unum in te est, alterum ex te pendet, si ita vixeris ut te omnes dignum quovis bono deputent.[36]

> [One quality is within you, but something far different emanates from you, when you so live that all people deem you a worthy man by whatever good you do.]

Decembrio sets before Frulovisi the humanist model of the virtuous man, in which the will is foremost and can help forestall any darker promptings.

Evidently Frulovisi took Decembrio's advice. In his later years he practiced medicine in Venice, the scene of his earlier disasters. Among his patients was the procurator of Saint Mark's, Lodovico Foscarini, and his family. Three of Foscarini's letters to Frulovisi survive, one of which complains of chronic migraines: *per plures dies magno capitis dolore*, he writes.[37] Over time Frulovisi became "un medico amicissimo del Foscarini."[38] These letters provide a last chronological reference point, 1456, for Frulovisi. By about 1465 he had probably passed from the scene.

In the dedication of the *Vita Henrici Quinti*, Frulovisi described Gloucester's encouragement and financial support, and then wrote, "From this comes a love of one's journey. From this come such zestful labors." [Hinc amor itineris. Hinc tanti labores].[39] As he continued on his way, he surely came to realize that financial reward and close association with princes could not by themselves stimulate a love of the journey or zest for his work. These must come ultimately from within. His realization brought him to a career that was less spectacular, with less access to the powerful than he had originally sought for himself. But it was one that conformed to Decembrio's paternal exhortation.

---

[36] Sabbadini, "Tito Livio Frulovisio," 81.

[37] Gianna Gardenal, "Lodovico Foscarini e la medicina," in *Umanesimo e rinascimento a Firenze e Venezia*, 3 vols. (Firenze: Leo S. Olschki Editore, 1983), 3.1: 254–56.

[38] Giovanni Battista Picotti, *Ricerche umanistiche*, Studi de lettere, storia e filosofia, 24 (Firenze: La Nuova Italia, 1955), 225n. Also idem, "Le lettere di Lodovico Foscarini," *l'Ateneo veneto*, 32.1 (1909): 47 n. 3.

[39] Frulovisi, *Vita*, 2.

PERCEPTIONS OF THE MAN

AND THE HUMANIST

As Remigio Sabbadini observes, Frulovisi had scant good fortune in the memory of posterity.[40] Simplistic judgments of him, whether as a man or a humanist, are easy to make, but invariably inadequate. In fact, he was both personally and professionally an individual of no little complexity.

In the early and middle years of his maturity, the personal Frulovisi was a man of mercurial temper who could hold a grudge with an almost grim intensity. To say so is both correct and incomplete. Haller's brief description tries to capture some of his variousness: a wanderer, interesting but unstable, curious and enigmatic.[41] C. W. Previté-Orton is more comprehensive in describing that complexity, perceiving him as a man of two aspects:

> He was quarrelsome, vain, presuming and extravagant. He was a bitter critic and satirist; he could never let an abuse or an enemy alone; he was born to make enemies and to wake long-lived feuds. But there is another side. He was independent, frank and courageous; he voiced high ideals of character and conduct; he had an unaffected admiration of nobility in thought and action, which implies some share of that nobility in him. He devoted himself with an almost reckless zeal to the cause of humanism, quitting certain profit in more humdrum pursuits, and at the risk of beggary. (xxxvi)

There was indeed a duality in him. Apparently, as long as Frulovisi actively pursued the humanist's profession, a personal balance, for whatever reason, eluded him. But once established in the practice of medicine, there grew in him over time a renewing equilibrium and, one would hope, a measure of personal satisfaction.

The fortunes of the professional Frulovisi were just as scant. Regarding scholarly response to Previté-Orton's *Opera Hactenus Inedita T. Livii Frulovisiis*, published in 1932, Walther Ludwig observes that:

> Although between 1932 and 1934 seven reviews [in four languages] emphatically stressed the importance of the publication for the study of the Renaissance and of the influence of antiquity as well as for the history of

---

[40] Sabbadini "Tito Livio Frulovisio," 55.
[41] Haller, *Piero da Monte,* *82 and n. 195.

the theatre and dramatic literature, later research has barely taken notice of it. ... It appears that no reader familiar with ancient literature has looked at the comedies.[42]

Little wonder. To begin with, textual survival and accessibility militated against his work being readily available and therefore more generally known. With regard to his poetry, for example, the *Encomium* survives in a single version, "a careless, ignorant copy, seemingly from a damaged original" at the end of MS. Cotton Claudius E. iii, following a later recopying of the text of the *Vita*.[43] Its first publication is in Previté-Orton's *Opera*. The *Humfroidos* also survives in a unique copy, the existence of which was not generally known until Roberto Weiss's passing allusion to it in a 1951 paper.[44] He dealt with it in more detail in 1957.[45] Of the three known Latin copies of the *De Republica*, one — Humphrey's copy donated to Oxford — is lost. Of the others, the copy in Italy, probably the presentation copy to Leonello d'Este, did not leave private collections until the late nineteenth century when Giuseppe Turri di Pellegrino (1802–1879) left it to the Biblioteca Municipale in Reggio Emilia. Its existence is first detailed in 1921.[46] The copy of the *De Republica* held in Spain was not widely known until 1989,[47] and again Previté-Orton's publication of the Reggio Emilia manuscript is the work's first. The 1716 printing of the *Vita Henrici Quinti*, edited by Thomas Hearne, has ironic aspects. Two copies contemporary to Frulovisi were and are extant, namely the Corpus Christi College, Cambridge MS. 285, illuminated by the artist of the comedies and Frulovisi's fair copy, and the College of Arms Arundel MS. 12, probably Humphrey's copy. Nevertheless, Hearne based his edition on the Cotton manuscript, copied later and somewhat corrupt.[48] And even though the unique copy of Frulovisi's plays was given to the library of St. John's College, Cambridge by Ilkiah Croke, M.D. in 1631, again it was not until

---

[42] Ludwig, "Humanistischer Dramatiker," 41.

[43] Previté-Orton, *Opera*, xix. B. L. MS. Cotton Claudius E. iii contains other histories and chronicles, as well as some letters. For its complete contents see its entry in Thomas Smith, *Catalogus Librorum Manuscriptorum Bibliothecae Cottoniae*, 1696; repr. ed. C. G. C. Tite; introductory essays trans. Godfrey E. Turton (Cambridge: D. S. Brewer, 1984), 44–45.

[44] Roberto Weiss, "New Light on Humanism in England in the Fifteenth Century," *Journal of the Warburg and Courtauld Institutes* 30 (1951): 21 n. 1.

[45] Weiss, "Humphrey," 220–27.

[46] Vincenzo Ferrari, *Studi di storia di letteratura e d'arte in onore di N. Campanini* (Reggio Emilia, 1921), 17–28. Six years earlier, Previté-Orton, in "The Earlier Career," 77, has just become aware of the title and knows of no extant copy.

[47] Kristeller, *Iter Italicum*, 4: 624.

[48] Previté-Orton, *Opera*, xviii, points out, however, that Hearne footnotes the superior readings of the Cambridge manuscript.

Previté-Orton's edition that they were published. These Latin comedies by an Italian playwright languished for three centuries in an English library.

Critical comment has on the whole been unfavorable to Frulovisi. In general, praise without qualification generally focuses on his "firsts": first portrayer of a Renaissance state, first humanist historian to write of events in England, first writer of comedies in the classical tradition actually to be performed.[49]

As a poet his reviews are not good. With respect to the *Encomium*, Previté-Orton gives him short shrift for

> ... his incapacity to write tolerable hexameters. The expression is tortuous and clumsy, the grammar dubious, the meaning, when discoverable, boastful and servile. (xxxv)

Alfredo Sammut calls it barren;[50] Sabbadini describes it as "substantially and formally wretched."[51] Of the *Humfroidos*, Weiss says that to call it mediocre would be "fulsome flattery."[52]

Of the two instances of his poetry, the *Encomium* on Stafford clearly shows itself unfinished. The rough text, marked with omissions and thrust into deeper disfavor by a careless copyist, may not even have been sent. Montanus's offer of employment could well have aborted this work in progress. In any case, to measure an unfinished draft against criteria appropriate to a polished work results in distortion and diverts attention from its real value. First, the *Encomium* provides significant bits of biographical information about Frulovisi at one of the most decisive points in his life; second, it shows him, a professional humanist, opting for a plausible strategy and an appropriate literary form to extricate himself from his predicament. [53]

On the other hand the *Humfroidos*, although it lacks polish, is finished enough to demonstrate Frulovisi's fondness for idiosyncratic Latin and to show him overmastered by the demands of the hexameter. Still, the choice of the panegyric form in this situation, like the dialogue a serviceable and favored genre for the human-

---

[49] See for example Previté-Orton, *Opera*, xxxvi; Haller, *Piero da Monte*, 26; King, *Venetian Humanism*, 378; St. John, "A Critical Edition," 1.

[50] Sammut, *Unfredo*, 19.

[51] Sabbadini, "Tito Livio Frulovisio," 59.

[52] Weiss, "Humphrey," 220.

[53] Paul Oskar Kristeller, *Eight Philosophers of the Italian Renaissance* (Stanford: Stanford University Press, 1969), 153, points out that, before such men began to be called humanists toward the late fifteenth century, they were usually referred to as poets, although many of them would hardly deserve the label "by modern standards."

ists, sets Frulovisi squarely among other working professionals and their writings: Francesco Filelfo and his *Sfortias*, Porcelio Pandone and his *Feltria*, and Tito Vespasiano Strozzi with his *Borseide*.[54] And despite its linguistic and formal flaws, it achieved the ends that Gloucester, who commissioned the work, had set for it: it helped him achieve a popularity that culminated in his favorable reception by parliament early in 1437.

Treatment of the *De Republica* is more congenial. Its extensive sources among the classics have already been mentioned. In addition it is an important link in the chain between Marsilio of Padua and Machiavelli.[55] Still, Maximilian Lehnerdt describes it as "literary but feeble."[56] Previté-Orton deals with the work in more detail. According to him, it makes no important contribution to the growth of modern political thought:

> It is a jejune production, in which fundamentals are not really discussed, and which but feebly handles even the practical construction of a constitution. At every step it betrays the humanist schoolmaster of the second rank. ... Yet its symptomatic value is considerable. We are in at the death in Italy of medieval theories of the state; we are at the transition from the instinctive policy of a medieval Italian commune to the state intentionally molded by its ruler in the fashion commended by Machiavelli ... and we are faced with a creditable example of the new humanistic standards of life and government divorced entirely and deliberately from ecclesiastical tradition. (xxx)

Frulovisi's use of the dialogue form for the *De Republica*, as has been seen, puts him in the ranks of knowledgeable working humanists. He employs living personages as characters, as Bruni had done in *Dialogi ad Petrum Histrum*; creates an atmosphere of open discourse, offering different positions on issues; and enriches the work with exempla and other allusions to the classics. His subject matter addresses issues of civil governance rather than ecclesiastical or theological concerns.

Most importantly, the work has much to tell about the shifting modes of development of the Italian states, so greatly in flux at this time. These observations in turn speak to Frulovisi's sensitivity to fundamental transformations, in, for example, the relationship between church and state. Weakened by Avignon and the Great Schism, the role of the church as plenipotentiary to the Christian

---

[54] Gransden, *Historical Writing*, 211.
[55] Stäuble, *Commedia umanistica*, 52; Sammut, *Unfredo*, 20; King, *Venetian Humanism*, 378.
[56] Lehnerdt, "Review," 161.

nations in temporal matters had entered upon its great decline. Reflecting the effect of that dynamic, some of the most critical underlying assumptions of the *De Republica* abandon the notion of the state as an instrument of eternal salvation in the hands of the church, and instead treat the church as one among many means of orderly governance available to the state.[57] Frulovisi presented the state as deliberately orchestrating these means to fashion itself through purposeful design rather than being fashioned by fortuitous evolution. He thus articulated in a humanistic literary mode what Jacob Burckhardt describes as a new fact appearing in history: "the State as the outcome of reflection and calculation, the State as a work of art."[58] Frulovisi was the earliest to grasp the complex dynamic of that reflection and calculation, and to record it in the literature of theories of the state.

Although Frulovisi textures the *De Republica* with the perspectives of his own experience — for example, the proper role and functions of the teacher — still, those experiences reflect the views of an ordinary citizen rather than a government functionary familiar with the apparatus and dynamics of power. By contrast, Machiavelli wrote *The Prince* after working for thirteen years in the Florentine chancery, bringing the kind of insight to his writing that would have benefited Frulovisi's work enormously.

The historical work, the *Vita Henrici Quinti*, succeeds solidly and without grave qualification, and is on the whole typical of the new learning. The medieval approach to history, in the process of being supplanted, was from one point of view moral philosophy teaching by example. In this context the historical writings of Petrarch are still preoccupied with classical biography. "Where better to cull examples of laudable conduct than from the idealized perfection of ancient times?"[59] Leonardo Aretino, in his *Historiae Florentini Populi* (1404), begins to look at the Dark Ages (a term of Petrarch's coinage) as the network of events and motives from which the Florence of his own day developed. He begins, in other words, to search the past for its political significance with respect to the present. In Flavio Biondo (1392–1463), called the first modern historian,[60] the moral

---

[57] Frulovisi evaluates religion, for example, in terms of its utility to the prince, who will be religious because religion is an aspect of justice, but who will be less religious than the common people. A prince's security, inspired by a fear of arms and punishment, is less desirable unless his people are stubborn or seditious. But there is a better way: "If [a prince] cultivates religion, then no one will plot against him. More than a prince's arms, one will fear a Defender God" [Si religionem colet, non machinabitur in illum quis. Super arma illius propugnatorem Deum quisque timebit] (362–63).

[58] Jacob Burckhardt, *The Civilization of the Renaissance in Italy*, trans. S. G. C. Middlemore (London: Harrap and Co., Ltd., 1929), 22.

[59] Gary Ianziti, *Humanistic Historiography under the Sforzas* (Oxford: Clarendon Press, 1988), 49–50.

[60] Jozef IJsewijn, *Companion to Neo-Latin Studies* (New York: North Holland Publishing Co., 1977), 48.

focus clearly yields primacy to the political. In treating contemporary Italian affairs he addresses the intricacies of political behavior, writes not only for an inner circle but also for statesmen and soldiers, and deals not simply with the flow of events but also with their causes. Frequently local princes needed to interpret events to their own advantage. As often as not they were, in Machiavelli's term, "new princes,"[61] men who came to power in the upheavals of the first part of the century. They attempted to justify a rule seized by force through an examination of recent history with its determining politics and military power.[62]

Thus a humanist history typically dealt with contemporary or near-contemporary events, was directed toward propagandistic ends often related to justifying a newly established dynasty, and took for its audience both the prince's closest advisers and, beyond them, senior members of diplomatic and military staffs. And so it was, for the most part, with the *Vita*. Frulovisi's work deals with Henry V's reign and particularly with his French campaigns and their political and military causes, for the purpose of glorifying his continental war policies and buttressing Gloucester's role in continuing those policies. It was addressed to the young Henry VI and would have been available to his advisers and senior administrators. Although the *Vita* was not directly intended to help legitimize the Lancastrian dynasty, its propagandistic bent is clear. Ralph Griffiths sees it as part of a broader strategy in which the *Libelle of Englysche Polycye* (1436) was aimed at the king's closest advisers, the *Vita* at a larger network of aristocratic readership, and various proclamations and ballads at a widely based audience.[63] And the appearance of the *Vita* (1438) came a century before Polydore Vergil (1470?–1555?) would publish his *Angliae Historiae* (1534–1555), a chronicle of special value to Henry VII and his new dynasty.

The quality of Frulovisi's writing in the *Vita* detracts somewhat from the work's overall success. His avidity for classical approaches is obvious, though not always in service to clarity, while syntax sometimes obfuscates. On the other hand, the orations he puts into the mouths of significant historical figures reconfirm his flair for dialogue.[64]

In 1442 Decembrio wrote Frulovisi that he had looked at the *Vita* with the utmost delight (*libentissime*); two decades later the Milanese chancellor paid the work the far more significant compliment of personally translating it into Italian

---

[61] Niccolò Machiavelli, *The Prince* (New York: New American Library, 1952), 118. This work of Machiavelli (1469–1532) was first published in 1537.

[62] Ianziti, *Humanistic Historiography*, 49–54. See also Gransden, *Historical Writing*, 210–13.

[63] Griffiths, *Henry VI*, 225.

[64] St. John, "A Critical Edition," 22–28. See also Blackwell, "Humanism and Politics," 431–35.

for inclusion in the Visconti-Sforza library.[65] He thus demonstrated a high level of critical acceptance for the work on behalf of the age in which it was produced.

Frulovisi's *Vita* would later influence the theatre. Raphael Holinshed, whose *Chronicles* served Shakespeare as a major source when he wrote *Henry the Fifth*, specifically cited the *Vita*, its anonymous English translation, and a separate adaptation that "hath followed the said Livius [i.e., Frulovisi] in the order of his books, as it were chapter for chapter." Unlike some modern critics, he praised the *Vita* for its "good, familiar and easie stile."[66] Walter G. Stone, in producing notes and an introduction to an edition of *Henry the Fifth*, "considered it might be interesting [to correlate] the original sources from which the *Chronicles* themselves were compiled." Wherever there is clear linkage between Frulovisi and Holinshed, he remarks it in a footnote.[67] Still, it is ironic that Frulovisi the historian rather than Frulovisi the dramatist influenced the theatre that came after him.

Before focusing more particularly on the comedies, it is interesting to note that the negative critical response garnered by Frulovisi generally arises from a detailed examination of his efforts in one specific genre or another. The judgment of Outi Merisalo, looking at the entire body of his work, stands in marked contrast. For Merisalo, Frulovisi shows himself typical of his age by varying vocabulary, morphology, and syntax according to whether he is writing comedy, history, or Ciceronian dialogue: "Frulovisi mastered several literary genres and varied his language accordingly, with the remarkable fluency of so many early Italian humanists, using the resources of the whole of Latinity."[68] This positive judgment of Merisalo's is allied to Holinshed's, two centuries earlier.

Although his Venetian comedies were all produced, apparently the plays Frulovisi wrote in England never made it to the stage. Space was left at the beginning of *Peregrinatio* and *Eugenius* to insert details of performance, as was done for the Venetian plays, but those spaces were never filled in for the comedies written in England.

Allusions to classical works are scattered throughout Frulovisi's plays, as will

---

[65] See J. H. Wylie, "Decembri's Version of the *Vita Henrici Quinti* by Tito Livio," *English Historical Review* 14 (1900): 84–89. Decembrio's 1463 translation is contained in MS. Vindobonensis 1610 at the Österreichische Nationalbibliothek in Vienna. Another MS. copy is held by the Biblioteca Apostolica Vaticana: Urbin. lat. 922, a microfilm of which is at the Vatican Film Library, Saint Louis University.

[66] Raphael Holinshed, *Chronicles*, ed. Henry Ellis (London: 1807–1808), 3: 136.

[67] William Shakespeare, *The Life of Henry the Fiftch*, with notes and an introduction by Walter George Stone (London: N. Trübner, 1880), i. The other sources were: Hall's *Chronicle*, Elmham's *Vita et Gesta Henrici Quinti*, the *Gesta Henrici Quinti*, Walsingham's *Historia Anglicana*, Monstrelet's *Chroniques*, and St. Remy's *Memoires*.

[68] Merisalo, "The Latin of Tito Livio," 668.

be shown in detail in the introduction and notes to *Peregrinatio.* His comedies have the humanist stamp throughout. They show their classical antecedents in Plautus, Terence and, for *Claudi Duo,* Lucian's dialogue *Timon.*[69]

Early critics have generally assumed that Frulovisi had no access to the Orsini codex and its twelve newly discovered plays of Plautus.[70] Richard Newald, for example, acknowledges the importance of Frulovisi's plays as the oldest examples of Latin school comedies in Italy and for the strong influence of Terence and Plautus, but adds that the newly discovered comedies of Plautus were still unknown to him.[71] Ludwig, however, holds otherwise, and demonstrates that Frulovisi, although he probably was unable to study the manuscript in any detail, had nevertheless read at least some of the newly discovered comedies. His narrative of the copying of the manuscript establishes opportunity:

Finally in the spring of 1431 [Orsini] gave it [the manuscript] to Lorenzo de Medici at Florence, where [Niccolò] Niccoli, between August 1431 and May 1432, could make an initial copy. Then through the intervention of Leonello d'Este the codex reached Ferrara. Guarino obtained it between the fifteenth and twenty-second of September 1432 and he likewise immediately copied the text of the hitherto unknown comedies. About the end of the year 1432 he sent this copy to Antonius Panormita. ... The original was back in the hands of Orsini by 1434 at the latest. [Frulovisi's] more detailed knowledge of the new plays by Plautus could have been acquired through the communicative Guarino, whose pupil Frulovisi had been. Or it might be that he was allowed to read Guarino's copy before it went to Panormita — in any case, in the late fall of 1432 Frulovisi could have had the opportunity to become acquainted with the new plays.[72]

---

[69] Padoan, "Commedia rinascimentale," 379–84. See also Stäuble, *Commedia umanistica,* 51, and Ludwig, "Humanistischer Dramatiker," 48–50.

[70] During the Middle Ages only eight comedies by Plautus were known: *Amphitryon, Asinaria, Aulularia, Captivi, Casina, Cistellaria, Curculio,* and *Epidicus.* In 1425 Nicholas of Cusa found a manuscript in the cathedral library of Cologne which contained four of the eight known works, plus twelve hitherto unknown plays: *Bacchides, Menaechmi, Mercator, Miles Gloriosus, Mostellaria, Persa, Poenulus, Pseudolus, Rudens, Stichus, Trinummus,* and *Truculentus.* For a narrative of the discovery and eventual dissemination of the manuscript, see Remigio Sabbadini, "Il Codice orsiniano di Plauto," in idem *Storia e critica di testi latini* (Firenze: G. C. Sansoni, 1967), 241–59; also Sandys, *Classical Scholarship,* 2: 34; for the place of the Orsini Codex among other source manuscripts for the works of Plautus see Reynolds, *Texts and Transmission,* 302–7.

[71] Richard Newald, "Livio, Tito, de Frulovisiis, *Opera Hactenus Inedita,*" in *A Bibliography of the Survival of the Classics* (London: The Warburg Institute, 1938), 2: 257.

[72] Ludwig, "Humanistischer Dramatiker," 42. Recalling that Frulovisi's first three comedies were written between September 1432 and August 1433 proves provocative in the context of this chronology.

Ludwig then looks at *Bacchides, Menaechmi, Mercator,* and *Miles Gloriosus,* the plays to which he believes Frulovisi was exposed, and he adduces some persuasive analogues. He points out some verbal parallels and then shows other dramaturgic similarities in additional plays. In *Emporia* Frulovisi names the intriguing slave Chrysolus; his counterpart in *Bacchides* is Chrysalus. The appearance of the *palla* in the *Menaechmi* is reflected in two Frulovisi works. In the seventh scene of *Claudi Duo,* Philaphrodita is in possession of a *palla* of the *meretrix,* Porna, while in scene three of *Peregrinatio* young Clerus escapes from the house of another Porna *meretrix,* clad only in her *palla.* The word *palla* does not appear in Terence, while in Plautus it is used four times in *Asinaria* and once each in *Mostellaria* and *Aulularia,* but over seventy times, Ludwig states, in *Menaechmi.*[73]

In general, Frulovisi seems to have taken great personal pleasure in his playwriting, comfortably orthodox with respect to the classical conventions in his first comedies, and later, without abandoning his basic rootedness, going beyond them. Even outside the scope of the comedies he gravitates toward the dialogue, as in the *De Republica* and the orations of the *Vita.* Contrasting this use of dialogue with his attempts at hexameters illuminates strengths and weaknesses. In addition, he begins with the *Peregrinatio* consciously to depart from the classical conventions of drama and frankly to experiment with form.

These experiments are foreshadowed in his departure from the Plautine model with respect to location. His first four plays are all laid in Italian cities: *Corallaria* in Pisa, *Claudi Duo* in Ravenna, and *Emporia* and *Symmachus* in Venice. Plautus invariably used some Greek city, and Frulovisi acknowledges his own departure from this convention in the argument to *Claudi Duo*: he states tongue in cheek that all Greek comic actors ply their trade in comedies laid in Athens, from which it follows that Pisans should be shown in Pisa and Ravennans in Ravenna (36). Thus his departure from the narrower aspects of the classical model.

But it is in *Peregrinatio* that he consciously pushes beyond the strictures of the unities of time and place. As Frulovisi states in the prologue:

Aliis nam Thessalonicae gesta, Venetiis vel Raven⟨n⟩ae, in Syria seu in Teucris, omnia uno in loco egimus. Veniebant oratores vel epistolae legebantur, facta quae narrarent aliis de longinquis locis. Nunc quae Rhodi gesta sunt narrantur Rhodi, quae Cretes Cretes. Similis in Britan⟨n⟩ico mos

---

[73] Ludwig, "Humanistischer Dramatiker," 43–44. See the seventy-two *Menaechmi* lemmata for *palla* in Gonzalez Lodge, *Lexicon Plautinum,* 2 vols. (Leipzig: Teubner, 1933; repr. Hildesheim: Olms, 1962), 2: 277. The word indeed does not appear in Patrick McGlynn, *Lexicon Terentianum,* 2 vols. (London and Glasgow: Blackie & Son, 1967).

est. Haec agetur coram: de praesentibus quasi sit acta vobis, cognoscere quod possitis quid ingenium valeat autoris. (188)

[Other writers describe actions at Thessalonica, Venice or Ravenna, in Syria or in Troy, but we show everything in one place. Others send in messengers or letters to narrate happenings in distant places. But now the things happening in Rhodes are described at Rhodes, in Crete at Crete. The custom is the same in Britain. Everything will happen right here: and when the action takes place, as it were, right in front of you, then you'll know how effective the author's inventiveness is.]

And he is as good as his word. In *Peregrinatio* the initial three scenes and the sixth are in Rhodes. Scenes four and five are in Britain, and the rest, seven through fifteen, are in Crete. Moreover, in the course of the play, time constraints give way as young Clerus sails from Rhodes to Crete, and again when Anapausis waits and watches for three days for a second glimpse of Clerus after his arrival in Crete. In his last play, *Eugenius*, all the action takes place in and around Ravenna, but the unity of time is again deliberately violated. During the course of the play Eugenius's father, Endoxus, sails from Ravenna, picks up the recently orphaned son of an old friend in another city, and returns. In addition, Eugenius at first resists marriage, then marries while his father is on his voyage, and subsequently is forced to divorce his wife when his father returns. Then at his father's command he marries a second woman, a shrew who eventually sours the father. Finally, Endoxus permits Eugenius to divorce the second wife and remarry the first. All of these events occur on an extended though unspecified time line, and Frulovisi for the most part presents them on stage.

He also begins deliberately to mix sad or serious subjects into his comedies. For Gloucester's benefit he states in the prologue of *Eugenius* that he labored:

... ut videas quantum de gravibus facete contendi possit. Fave coeptis suis, optime princeps. Ridicula et nova res est, plurimum permixta gravibus. (224)

[... so that you should see to what degree it is possible to treat humorously these grave affairs. Favor these undertakings, best of princes. The play is funny and fresh, with a full mix of serious concerns.]

Indeed Ludwig describes *Eugenius* as "eine Liebeskomödie in ein allegorisches Spiel."[74]

---

[74] Ludwig, "Humanistischer Dramatiker," 61.

The funny and the serious mix together in scene three when young Eugenius, fearful of marriage and desirous of giving himself to scholarship without the inevitable distractions of a family, debates Endoxus and other old men about the advantages and disadvantages of the married state. Thematically this scene is related to the *De Re Uxoria* (1415) of Francesco Barbaro (1390–1454) and the *An Seni Sit Uxor Ducenda* (c. 1435) of Poggio. Theatrically, Endoxus's three senescent advisers come straight from Terence's *Phormio*.[75] In *Eugenius*, however, the young man's trepidation and Endoxus's demand that he marry put a comic cast on an essentially serious subject. Later, in scene eleven, Endoxus returns from his journey by sea with Stephanus, his new ward, the son of his recently deceased old friend. He goes on at length about the friendship and love he shared with Stephanus's father, and on the nature of death in general and of his own in particular, which he says is waiting in the wings. It is a quite serious though amiable interlude that does not move the action of the comic plot at all. Moreover, its gravity shows a dimension and complexity in the character of Endoxus that actually impinges upon his earlier single-mindedness and simplicity, and detracts from the comic effect. These two aspects of Endoxus sometimes feel like two different characters, and at times work against the play's success.

There is a mix of the amusing and the sad in *Peregrinatio* as well. In scene four, Clerus's mother Erichea in Britain laments her fate, having married Clerus's father and then been abandoned while pregnant. Now, to find his father, Clerus has also left her, and she is alone and waiting to die. Later standards might consider this scene of deliberate pathos, nested in an otherwise straightforward comedy, to be out of place. Nor does the scene move the plot, except to terminate Rhystes's bigamy. Erichea could have been deceased when the curtain first rose and the play's outcome would not have been changed. But this scene does illustrate Frulovisi's willingness to challenge assumptions about how a play ought to be constructed. Moreover, it establishes a darker melancholy to contrast with the lighter, charming melancholy of Anapausis in scene eight as she tells her nurse that she has fallen in love.

The scenes with Clerus's mother also illustrate another departure from classical models. In general, women characters did not often appear on the Roman comic stage, and when they did, they were most frequently mercenary *meretrices* or harridan wives. Respectable women were relatively infrequently presented, and only in minor roles. Another example of Frulovisi's evolutionary use of female characters

---

[75] See particularly ll. 348–358.

occurs in a scene in *Peregrinatio* between young Anapausis and her maidservant Elpis. The girl feels sick and describes her symptoms. Elpis figures out that she is in love, and they plot how to find the young man, whom she saw once for about a minute in front of her house, and how to persuade her parents to let her wed him. The scene charms Sabbadini, who says he can find no certain model for it in Latin comedy.[76] Indeed the scene it most resonates with is forward in time almost two centuries, to Juliet and her nurse.

Still another example of pushing beyond the boundaries of expected female character limitations shows in the use of Elpis as a type of the clever slave. *Peregrinatio* has two such characters: Aristopistes, who spends his onstage time trying to extricate himself from his predicaments; and Elpis, who actually carries out the classic function of the clever slave and helps bring off the marriage of Anapausis and Clerus. In the denouement, however, only Aristopistes receives his freedom, while Elpis simply drops from sight. Finally there is Anapausis herself. In having to overcome obstacles to gain her beloved, she thus performs the function normally reserved for the moonstruck young man, while Clerus spends most of his time bemoaning his fiscal fate and general lack of good fortune.

So Frulovisi, solidly in the middle of a movement characterized in part by its imitation of the classics, demonstrates in his later plays a willingness, even an eagerness, to experiment with his approaches to comedy and to challenge dramaturgic assumptions. He deliberately violates the unities, mixes the sad and the serious, and exceeds his models in the functions and texturing of women's characters. He thus shows himself a playwright who consciously pushes beyond traditional boundaries, although by modern standards he sometimes misses the mark.

Frulovisi's occasional dramaturgic ineptness rests to a large degree on a collective lack of experience in the age. The modern theatre did not as yet exist, and in fact Frulovisi's efforts were a significant part of a growing movement to invent and define such a theatre. What remains is that Frulovisi, in choosing a humanist venue at least partly for his own creative pleasure, hit upon comedy and succeeded at it in solid, journeyman fashion. H. L. St. John's observation with regard to his Latin in the *De Republica* seems appropriate also to his later comedies, namely that his enthusiasm "pushed him ahead to the point where he found few masters and models."[77] Previté-Orton offers a kindred observation:

---

[76] Sabbadini, "Tito Livio Frulovisio," 72.
[77] St. John, "A Critical Edition," 22.

He had to make a theatre and a method with all the blunders and inca-
pacity that belong to a first attempt without a teacher or the stored-up
capital of practical experience to guide him. (xxxv–xxxvi)

In viewing his work overall one can say that, although his use of language and
control of form were sometimes not centered, Frulovisi brought an originality into
his imitation of classical models and worked assiduously at his craft. ""His stuffed
and stopped-up brain' reached at times to new conceptions denied to contempora-
ries of greater genius. ... He had a true dramatic talent. ... He foreshadowed
much that greater men were to do." (xxxv–xxxvi)

THE PLAY

Peregrinatio follows the fortunes of young Clerus. When the play begins, he has left
his home and his mother in Britain, along with his slave Aristopistes, and is on
the island of Rhodes trying to find his father Rhystes. Many years before,
Rhystes, while traveling, had met Clerus's mother Erichea and fallen in love with
her. The young woman, wealthy and independent, insisted upon marriage. Soon
after the ceremony Rhystes abandoned his new wife, knowing she was pregnant.
She would never tell her son anything about his father, so Clerus has set off with
his slave and a goodly amount of cash to search the Mediterranean for him.

On Rhodes Clerus becomes smitten with the beautiful *meretrices* who specialize
in travelers, and to protect their funds from foolish spending he gives all the
money to Aristopistes to safeguard. No sooner done than he falls into the
clutches of Porna the *meretrix*, and since he can't pay for her services he is forced
to escape from her establishment in one of her outfits. To make matters worse,
the sobersided Aristopistes has been arrested on trumped-up charges and their
money confiscated. Clerus is forced for the moment to abandon his Aristopistes,
and escape from Rhodes to Crete.

Back in Britain Erichea has become ill, and it is clear her prognosis is dubious
at best. Meanwhile, Aristopistes cons his jailer Lorarius into thinking he's a member of the Belgian nobility, and that his father will shower Lorarius with wealth
and position if he gets Aristopistes out of this fix and back home. They too head
for Crete where Aristopistes says he's deposited large sums with a banker.

After he left Britain, Rhystes returned to his home on Crete and soon con-
tracted a bigamous marriage to a young widow, Epiichis. At the same time, he became the stepfather of his second wife's daughter, Anapausis. But Rhystes is eaten
up by guilt at his abandonment of Erichea, and his second marriage is not a

happy one. Moreover, he has sent abroad his steward, Presbites, to conduct important business and search for his son. Presbites returns to tell his master that Erichea has died and his son, present whereabouts unknown, has set out with a slave to find his father. On top of this bad news, Presbites reports that the trip's commercial mission has been a failure as well. Rhystes blames these calamities on the gods, who must be punishing him for his bad deeds years before in Britain.

In the meantime, Anapausis is just reaching the age of marriage. She confides to her maid Elpis that she has fallen instantly in love with a young stranger who paused for a minute in front of the house. Elpis agrees to find out who he is and convince her parents to let her marry him. Meanwhile Aristopistes arrives on Crete with his jailer, and they link up with an agent of Rhystes who is seeking the old man's son. At the same time in another part of the city, Rhystes by chance meets Clerus, likes the young man, and offers to marry him to Anapausis. He brings Clerus home, and the young man turns out to be Anapausis's mysterious beloved. Elpis persuades Epiichis to let her daughter marry, and Aristopistes, at last released from his chains, is given his freedom as part of the wedding celebration.

Frulovisi's concept for the set of this boy-meets-girl comedy probably involved a single house fronting on a street. His comedy actually presents three houses, but sequentially rather than simultaneously: Porna's house in the Rhodes scenes; the house of Clerus's mother Erichia in Britain; and the house of Rhystes in Crete.

Two of the Crete scenes, eight and twelve, seem to involve the use of something like an inner above for Anapausis's bedroom. Perhaps *Asinaria*, much in evidence in *Peregrinatio*, gave Frulovisi the idea for an interior scene. This play of Plautus has an indoor father-son debauching scene which is observed by the audience, apparently through the door into the procuress's house. During the scene, sustained conversation is clearly comprehensible from within. On the other hand, the idea may have come from Frulovisi's visits to play performances in England. We know he attended theatrical presentations during his stay there because, in discussing his conscious violation of the unity of place in the prologue of *Peregrinatio*, he remarks that "the custom is the same in Britain" [Similis in Britan‹n›ico mos est].

In any case, lines of dialogue in scene twelve support the idea of a space "inside" the house, conceived as an inner above. Anapausis's mother Epiichis, apparently in the space representing Anapausis's room, calls for Elpis, who likely enters on the street. When Epiichis tells her that Anapausis is ill, Elpis says she'll cure her. "Then run," the mother replies. "Climb those stairs" [Igitur curre. Conscende gradus]. "And you come down" [Et tu descende], Elpis responds. A few lines later in this same scene, when Anapausis believes she hears Clerus's voice, she tells

Elpis, "Open that window" [Detege illam fenestram],[78] firmly locating the action "within." Given such verbal prompts, this translation, including interpolated stage directions, assumes an inner above with its stairway located backstage and out of sight of the audience.

The double entendres with which Frulovisi invests *Peregrinatio* fall predominantly though not exclusively in scene two with Porna the *meretrix*. *Venus* receives perhaps the most attention, meaning as it does both the goddess of love and the sexual act. The playwright builds on this ambiguity with certain forms of the verb *venire*, to come, which has the same sexual meaning as its English counterpart when prefixed with *per-* (literally, "to arrive"). *Servire*, "to serve," and *officium*, "duty," also have sexual connotations that Frulovisi puts to use.[79] These varied terms sometimes provide humor as unintended sexual innuendo: *Non possum esse tecum*, Clerus for example tells Porna. *Servum convenero*: "I can't be with you. I'm hooking up with my slave." The sexual ambiguity of *convenero* can imply a more intimate relationship between master and slave than Clerus intended. In addition, Frulovisi provides an interesting contrast between the callow and for the most part accidental sexual humor of Clerus and his slave Aristopistes, and that of Porna the *meretrix*. Her final lines in scene two are deliberate and graphic, and evoke a kind of shocked surprise as much as laughter.

Dialogue parallels to both Plautus and Terence are frequent. Of the approximately one hundred noted instances cited, Plautus garners a little more than sixty percent, while Terence accounts for the remainder. All six of the Terentian comedies are represented. In particular, *Adelphoe*, *Phormio*, and *Eunuchus* make significant showings. A few examples suffice to show Frulovisi's knowledge of Terence:

Peregrinatio	Terence
Me tibi commendo. Tu es patronus, tu magister, tu pater, tuus ego sum totus. (sc. 3)	In te spes omnis, Hegio, nobis sitast: te solum habemus, tu es patronus, tu pater. (*Adelphoe* 455–456)
Sed cesso ad uxorem meam pergere, quae me plus amat quam oculos suos. (sc. 7)	Ni magis te quam oculos nunc amo meos (*Adelphoe* 701); Qui te amat plus quam hosce oculos. (*Adelphoe* 903)

---

[78] Another plausible rendering is "Throw open that shutter."

[79] For a discussion of *servio* and *officium* in this context see J. N. Adams, *The Latin Sexual Vocabulary* (Baltimore: Johns Hopkins University Press, 1982), 163–64; for *pervenio*, 144.

Infelix et infortunatus homo, virtute quamvis ornatus satis. (sc. 10)	Sic possiderem, ornatus esses ex tuis virtutibus. (*Adelphoe* 176)
Ignavos et timidos, non fortes, laedit; iuvat potius. (sc. 1)	Fortis fortuna adiuvat. (*Phormio* 203)
Montes huic ego pollicebor auri. (sc. 2)	Modo non montis auri pollicens. (*Phormio* 68)
Si res digna sit, cui te nervos intendas tuos. (sc. 8)	Sic adeo digna rest, ubi tu nervos intendas tuos. (*Eunuchus* 312)

Also pervasive are convergences with Plautus, most frequently among the eight longer known comedies, less so among the twelve new plays in the Orsini codex.[80] *Asinaria* is a significant presence. It is the source for the birding metaphor which Frulovisi uses for the *meretrices* in scenes one and two, as well as for "Man is a wolf to a man" in scene three. *Asinaria* also contains a sequence where the master is trying to get his money back from his slave, a scene duplicated in scene one of *Peregrinatio*, roles reversed, as Aristopistes tries to get his master Clerus to give him the money. In addition, Frulovisi, as mentioned, probably based his staging concept for Anapausis's room on Plautus's presentation of the debauching scene.

Amphitryon, one of the eight longer known works, provides the basis for Clerus's oath, *per supremi regis regna iuro*, in scene ten, and for the list of places Lorarius searches as he tries to find Arisopistes in scene eleven. A similar list appears in *Epidicus*, also one of the longer known comedies, but this latter play has only a few minor convergences throughout *Peregrinatio*, making *Amphitryon* Frulovisi's most likely source. From *Captivi* come numerous borrowings, including Clerus's "clothed with virtue"; Epiichis's wish, "I'd rather the children be alive though beggars"; and most particularly in the final scene, "Human fortune rules us: it squeezes us to favor us."

Ten of the twelve new comedies in the Orsini codex have parallels in *Peregrinatio*, but they are only a few and not particularly significant. Often they echo similar passages in the longer known comedies or in Terence, or they appear widely in many places in the literature and hence are possibly coincidental.

---

[80] See note 70.

Frulovisi, then, had a good familiarity with Terence and the longer known eight plays of Plautus, and used them freely as sources for *Peregrinatio*. He had a more generalized familiarity with the newly discovered comedies of the Orsini manuscript, and the less frequent and significant convergences with these plays in the dialogue of *Peregrinatio* leave tentative the conclusion that he knew these works in any detail. He had probably read some of them, although it is unlikely he studied them at length.

Themes of fortune are woven throughout *Peregrinatio*, particularly in the person of Clerus, and are often rooted in classical sources. Even his name has relevance to this motif: in a gloss Frulovisi explains that the word's Greek source, κλῆρος, translates into Latin as *sors*, a lot used in gambling. Clerus's life, then, is like a pair of dice in his own hands. The young man is a conscious follower of *Fortuna*: "Fortune's the goddess for me." But for a time his physical promptings make Venus a viable competing divinity. Aristopistes cautions Clerus against a switch of allegiance, but he is young and overconfident: "That'll never happen." Inevitably a brief schism ensues, and he falls into the clutches of one of the *meretrices*. Proselitus, a good Samaritan character, tells him in scene three that the wheel of fortune which has cast him down will continue to turn and raise him up. In scene ten Clerus does some stocktaking and resolves: "Let it be as Fortune wills" [fiat quod fortuna velit]. Such an acceptance of fortune is typical of Terence, for example at *Phormio* 138: "what fortune's bouncing ball brings, let's carry calmly" [quod fors feret feremus aequo animo]. Clerus's recommitment to the goddess initiates the play's denouement, for before the scene ends Rhystes has offered him the hand of his daughter Anapausis in marriage. In the final scene Clerus repeats the substance of what the good Samaritan had told him: "You see? Human fortune rules us: it squeezes us to favor us" [Viden? Fortuna humana nos regit: artat ut lubet]. This articulation of the theme of fortune comes directly from Plautus, at *Captivi* 304: "Sed viden? Fortuna humana fingit artatque ut lubet."

But Frulovisi's borrowings from classical models are not limited to the motif of fortune. In fact, the dozens of links in *Peregrinatio* to Plautus, Terence, and other ancient authors fall across a broad spectrum of motifs and themes. Sometimes these links are quite obvious, sometimes they are subtly disguised. Moreover, Frulovisi was not unusual in borrowing from those who had gone before. Most humanist writers would as a matter of course weave the thoughts, style, and even the very words of ancient writers into their work. They referred to this technique as *imitatio*, and how well an author applied it in his writings had a significant influence on critical judgments concerning the excellence of his work.

On one level, *imitatio* merely involves the manipulation of words. Gasparino Barzizza (1370–1431), in his *De Imitatione*, recommended to his students such techniques as adding, deleting, or transposing words, substituting synonyms, or producing some verbal alteration in, for example, number, case, tense, or voice.[81] Frulovisi mastered this approach, as has been seen, but the most satisfying *imitatio* reached well beyond such a rudimentary level.

The ancients themselves had evolved a set of norms for their own *imitatio*, and their approach proved attractive to humanists. The object imitated must be worth imitating; the spirit rather than the letter should be reproduced; the imitation must be tacitly acknowledged, on the understanding that the reader will recognize and approve the borrowing; what is borrowed must be made one's own by individual treatment and assimilation to its new place and purpose; and the imitator must think of himself as competing with his model, even if he knows he cannot win.[82] Clearly the nature and complexity of *imitatio* is much more dynamic and multilayered than Barzizza's simplistic verbal approach.

The generic concept of *imitatio*, for example, can be divided into following (*sequi*), imitating (*imitari*), and emulating (*aemulari*). Yet the borders among these different species of *imitatio* cannot always be unequivocally defined. They are "versions, not hard and fast categories with immutable boundaries."[83] To illustrate this lack of sharp definition in humanist thinking about *imitatio*, following can be thought of as nontransformative, merely the gathering of passages from another author — yet with some changes of words, in the manner Barzizza recommends. Imitating, the second type of *imitatio*, involves a modifying process in which "the transformation is strong,"[84] and the changes are in at least as great relief as the similarities. Finally, at the level of emulating, modification can be refined to such a degree that the connection of an author's work to its models virtually disappears, his effort thus becoming dissimulative.

This masking of sources would seem in one sense a mark of success within the framework of *imitatio*. Yet in another sense it conflicts with the idea of vying with one's model. When one competes, one can at first follow in the footsteps of the model; then later, by dint of much work, draw abreast of him; or even, as the culmination of the competition, surpass the model in literary excellence. But if, in its transformation, one's source has been masked with such artifice that it is no longer apparent, who will realize that the author has exceeded his model in excel-

---

[81] See the section on Barzizza in Martin L. McLaughlin, *Literary Imitation in the Italian Renaissance* (Oxford: Clarendon Press, 1995), 103–6.

[82] D. A. Russell, "De Imitatione," in *Creative Imitation and Latin Literature*, ed. David West and Tony Woodman (Cambridge: Cambridge University Press, 1979), 16.

[83] G. W. Pigman III, "Versions of Imitation in the Renaissance," *Renaissance Quarterly* 33 (1980): 32.

[84] Pigman, "Versions of Imitation," 32.

lence? The connection, then, must be even more highly refined, apparent upon reflection at least to the learned. And the apprehension of these filigree connections
becomes for the learned a major aspect of their reading enjoyment. An author
who thus pleases such *docti* might be described, in Seneca's words, as a *magni vir
ingenii* who impresses his own form on what he draws from others.[85]

On the other hand, a failed attempt at *imitatio* often meant a transformation of
the original so shallow as to be negligible, with the source glaringly obvious to the
reader. To Petrarch, such an author had merely aped his model, earning himself
the epithet *simia*.[86] Or alternatively he would be called a thief, and "theft belongs
to the vocabulary of failed transformation and is used to attack."[87] For Jacopo
Langosco, then, to view *Corallaria* as a theft and to refer to its author as *fur* means
that he considered Frulovisi not just a plagiarist but a failed writer. Frulovisi's po-
lemic vehemence in response is much more understandable in the context of *imitatio*.

But the larger question about Frulovisi concerns the ways in which he attempted *imitatio* in his own comedies. At the level of dialogue his efforts are more
or less obvious, with numerous verbal ties to Plautus and Terence. These parallels
are cited in the body of the play, with footnotes providing the Latin models from
Roman comedies.

These citations do not, however, prove that Frulovisi sat down and searched
the texts of Roman comedies for each and every borrowing, and then, mindful of
Barzizza's recommendations, copied the dialogue with variations. Still, sometimes
this appears to be exactly what happened. The flurry of citations at the beginning
of *Peregrinatio*'s final scene, for example, seems such an instance. Here Frulovisi is
carefully tying together themes of fortune and acceptance of one's fate with his
characters' final situations.

But what these dialogic parallels, instances of *imitatio*, demonstrate with certain-
ty is Frulovisi's thorough immersion in the fictional world and words of Roman
comedy. These demonstrations start with the prologue's ritual plea for quiet and
a fair hearing and extend all the way to the request for applause at the play's end.
A verbal homage to Plautus's characteristic wordplay is Frulovisi's use in scene
nine of *medioxissimi*, a playful word employed by the Roman in *Cistellaria* (*medioxumi*). In *Peregrinatio*'s context it means the extremest point of right-in-the-middle-

---

[85] Quoted by Pigman, "Versions of Imitation," 5 n. 7.

[86] Thomas M. Greene quotes Petrarch's letter to Boccaccio: one's writing should "resemble the
original without reproducing it. ... We may use another man's conceptions and the color of his style,
but not his words. ... The first procedure makes poets, the second makes apes.": "Petrarch and the
Humanist Hermeneutic," in *Italian Literature: Roots and Branches*, ed. Giose Rimanelli and Kenneth John
Atchity (New Haven: Yale University Press, 1976), 211–12. The translation is Morris Bishop's.

[87] Pigman, "Versions of Imitation," 15.

ness, and that is precisely where Frulovisi's use of *imitatio* situates him with respect to the comedies of Plautus and Terence.

Sometimes a speech with a verbal parallel resonates with the ancients on a philosophical level as well. In his introspective soliloquy which opens scene ten, Clerus first summarizes his difficult situation, then decides to roll with the punch:

> Si non potero quod volo, volam quod potero. Nequeo meo modo vivere? Vivam alieno.

> [If I can't do what I want, I'll want what I can do. I can't live the way I'd like? Then I'll live a different way.]

Its verbal parallel, duly noted, comes from *Andria* 305–6:

> Quoniam non potest id fieri quod velis, / id velis quod possit.

> [Since what you want can't be done, you should want what can.]

It is reiterated at 805:

> Ut quimus, aiunt, quando ut volumus non licet.

> [We do the doable, as they say, when what we want's against the rules.]

All of this clearly demonstrates verbal *imitatio*. But an entirely different instance of *imitatio* obtains simultaneously on another level. Clerus wraps up his "I'll want what I can do" sequence thus: "Well, let Fortune work it out" [Fiat quod Fortuna velit]. Such stoic acceptance is a recurring motif in Terence, and Frulovisi has adopted this outlook as a significant theme of his play. In the context of light, romantic comedy it is an amiable stoicism, in some ways even shallow, for fate in this genre inevitably provides a happy ending. Its pithiest expression in Terence is at *Phormio* 138: "What Fortune's bouncing ball brings, let's carry calmly" [Quod fors feret feremus aequo animo]. This terse recapitulation in *Phormio* has some glancing alliterative ties to the dialogue of scene ten, but the philosophical links are much more basic, and serve *imitatio* much more trenchantly.

As mentioned earlier, *Asinaria* contains a sequence where the master is trying to get his money back from his slave, a routine Frulovisi used in scene one of *Peregrinatio*, roles reversed, with Aristopistes trying to get his master Clerus to give him the money. Clearly an instance of *imitatio*, such a role reversal seems the situational equivalent of Barzizza's tinkering with the surface form of words.

As the final curtain approaches, the *meretrix* in *Asinaria* says, "Remember the

coat" [De palla memento]. Frulovisi does indeed remember, in the process providing another instance of *imitatio*, this time involving costumes. At the beginning of
scene three, Clerus escapes from Porna's house dressed in clothing he has stolen
from her. Clearly, though, this entrance of Clerus is much more directly related to
that of Menaechmus of Syracuse, who comes on stage from Erotium's house
wearing her *palla*, which he intends to steal — and the *Menaechmi* is one of the
twelve plays discovered later.

In another instance of serving *imitatio* through situation, Rhystes in *Peregrinatio*
is a bigamist with a son by a woman he married in England; she dies there during
the course of the play. In the denouement, that son marries Rhystes's stepdaughter, the child his second wife brought with her into their new family. In Terence's
Phormio, Chremes also has an out-of-town wife who years before had given birth
to their daughter. As the curtain rises, mother and child have come to Athens to
find him. At virtually the same instant that Chremes's nephew falls in love at first
sight with his daughter, the girl's mother dies. The play concludes with the fathers
of both young people consenting after the fact to their marriage. Audience members familiar with Terence would very likely recognize the situation, with Frulovisi's modifications, and take added pleasure in his play because of this *imitatio*.

One of Frulovisi's most innovative instances of *imitatio*, and one which shows
him clearly making his borrowings his own, is his division of the stock character
of the clever slave into two separate people, one of whom is a woman. Aristopistes passes his onstage time trying to extricate himself from his difficulties, while
Elpis puts all of her efforts into trying to find the boy her mistress has fallen
madly in love with. This splitting of a type into two characters is not unique —
it sometimes happened when a Roman play resulted from *contaminatio*, the melding
of more than one Greek original into a single new work. What is unusual is to
have both a slave and a lover be women, and to have them spend extended time
onstage being respectively clever and moonstruck. This instance of Frulovisi's *imitatio* is firmly rooted in his sources, yet simultaneously reaches beyond them.

This observation must inevitably bring up the question of competition. Did
Frulovisi decide not merely to walk in the footsteps of Plautus and Terence, but
attempt to come abreast of them and even try to surpass them? If so, his strategy
seems to have been to try to exceed his models while still retaining a recognizable
connection to their works. The stock characters of the moonstruck lover and the
clever slave are obvious links, but Frulovisi, in writing them as women, has clearly
reached beyond his sources. In another instance in *Phormio*, mentioned earlier, Terence has the mother of one of the lovers die. Although this woman never appears
onstage, Frulovisi brings Clerus's failing mother Erichia into two scenes. And
while he does not show her actual death, he can still be thought of as having

pushed beyond his model. Finally, the debate in *Eugenius* about remaining single, between the title character on one side and his father and three advisers on the other, derives from Terence's *Phormio* with its own title character debating Demipho and his three advisers about the marriage of Demipho's son. Here Frulovisi's attempt to surpass his model lies in his use of a *roman à clef* mechanism: the playwright has deliberately made Eugenius the figure of his patron Humphrey, and states as much in the prologue.

If Frulovisi attempted to surpass his models, did he succeed? The use of female characters as clever slave and lover is clearly innovative, and if innovation constitutes superiority over one's models then here Frulovisi earns the laurel. On the other hand, bringing Clerus's dying mother onstage seems only an excursion into nascent melodrama, while the mingling of the fictional Eugenius with the personage of his patron seems less a successful competition than a stratagem of flattery. True, one is rightly impressed with some aspects of Frulovisi's treatment of female characters. But overall, his competitive efforts seem not quite to succeed.

Still, Frulovisi appears to view the quality of his writing as consistently high. In its prologue he recommends his sixth play *Peregrinatio* to his readers, in part because "the other plays have been pleasing to the learned" [gratae fuerunt doctis aliae]. This claim implies that the *docti* who read his work will detect subtle connections to his sources and derive intellectual enjoyment from them. Moreover, in the same prologue he states that when the viewer beholds the action of the play, "he'll be able to see how effective is the inventiveness of the author" [cognoscere quod possitis quid ingenium valeat autoris]. Predicating *ingenium* of himself evokes Seneca's *magni vir ingenii*, and implies that Frulovisi considered himself as striving within the dynamic of *imitatio*.

At this point a closer examination of Frulovisi from a feminist perspective is appropriate. It is true that he broke with the past in putting significant female characters on stage as mother, clever slave, and lover. Notwithstanding, if one looks in his plays for the attitudes of his age toward women, one will not be disappointed. Porna the *meretrix*, for example, is an interchangeable character, mercenary and manipulative, and indeed appears with the same name in an earlier Frulovisi comedy. In another place, a line of the curmudgeonly Rhystes depends for its relevance on the stereotype of the harridan wife: "This is the nature of women: they aren't conquered by sweet-talking them — it takes harsh words and confrontations" [Hoc est ingenium mulierum: asperis et contrariis, non adulationibus vincuntur].[88] And Erichea, lamenting her fate, says, "What happiness can

---

[88] See Terence, *Eunuchus* 812–13: Novi ingenium mulierum: / nolunt ubi velis, ubi nolis cupiunt ultro.

there be for a woman, if she is separated from her husband" [Quid beatitudinis esse potest mulieri, a viro si separata sit]? Moreover, Frulovisi puts a statement about gender as diminishment into the mouth of one of the women, who takes the truth of it for granted. "Even though our sex makes us frail," Dynamis sympathizes with Erichea, "keep your heart calm and constant" [Quanquam sexus istud nobis afferat labilitatis, animo bono fac sies et constanti].

Frulovisi, then, is no enlightened fifteenth-century champion of women. Rather, he is a true artist in the sense that unexpected insights, both pointed and pleasing, arise from his natural empathy with characters of both genders, over and above the customary stock characterizations which constitute a playwright's short-cuts to laughter in this genre.

Peregrinatio is a pleasant and amusing piece clearly exhibiting the humanistic imitation of classical comedy, and at the same time it is more than that. Gilbert Norwood applies the term auto-*contaminatio* to Molière because the French playwright, while adapting Plautus's *Amphitryon*, included a scene from one of his own earlier plays.[89] The term is applicable to Frulovisi as well, for as he assembled a collection of incident, character, and dialogue from Plautus and Terence, he also incorporated scenes of his own making which centered on Clerus's mother.

But in its comic situations, dialogue, and putative staging the play is unequivocally a stepchild of Plautus and Terence. Still, while maintaining its links to its models, the work attempts to reach beyond them within the context of *imitatio*. It selectively employs double entendre and lays down the theme of fortune in a satisfying way. And against an expected background of sexual stereotypes the play shows flashes of insight into the situation of women, and presents female characters in surprising, sympathetic, and important ways.

Peregrinatio has been constructed in competent journeyman fashion by one of the groundbreaking playwrights of the early humanist theatre. After a delay approaching six centuries, it richly deserves a life on the stage.

THE TRANSLATION

As Previté-Orton earlier, I have let stand in the Latin text most of Frulovisi's usages unremarked — single letters for diphthongs (-*e* for -*ae*) for instance, or an occasional elision of the genitive plural (-*um* for -*ium*). It should be noted that such usages are not always consistent. Where I thought it best to correct or clari-

---

[89] Gilbert Norwood, *The Art of Terence* (Oxford: Basil Blackwell: 1923), 16.

fy, I have employed angle brackets or footnotes. In addition, I have reproduced unaltered Previté-Orton's Greek, which in turn derives from Frulovisi's.

Frulovisi set down virtually no stage directions; those given in the translation within square brackets are mine. In addition, in scene eleven a page of the manuscript is missing, and I have provided notional dialogue to bridge this gap.

At the head of most scenes, Frulovisi noted the Greek words from which he derived characters' names, and set down their meanings in Latin. I provide translations of these glosses in footnotes.

Roberto Weiss once observed that a medieval translation tended to be word-for-word, while a humanist rendering was preoccupied with concepts and ideas.[90] In this sense, I have tried to make the translation of *Peregrinatio* firmly humanist. Beyond that, I have been at pains to weave through the whole a colloquial thread, and simultaneously to push the work toward both that Plautine be-all and end-all, laughter, and those Terentian accompaniments, the pleasurable chuckle, the knowing smile. At the same time, I have labored to stay within the boundaries of translation and avoid slipping across the border into the more indulgent terrain of adaptation.

As usual in this kind of enterprise, the effort must inevitably fall short. Occasionally an instance of Frulovisi's wordplay refused to carry across into English. Conversely, I sometimes found the translation gravitating naturally into, for example, playful alliteration, although there was none in the Latin. As a case in point, Aristopistes's "non despero quin fortassis talem sortem potiare, ut patriam tuam omnino flocifacias" in scene one becomes "I don't worry that you'll come under the power of some fatal fate, or that you'll throw off your homeland and hearthside altogether."

Once or twice it made sense to interpolate a bit more than lay in the original. In scene ten, for instance, Rhystes asks Clerus his name and the boy responds, "Penthon." The Greek etymology was important to Frulovisi, and to make the name's meaning clear within the framework of Rhystes's character and the scene's momentum, I inserted, "Mr. Gloom, eh? An undertaker's name," before Frulovisi's "You'll laugh more often with me, son. Be happy." To which Clerus replies, "Quod possum, facio" — "I do the possible." Words for any translator to live by.

---

[90] Roberto Weiss, *The Spread of Italian Humanism* (London: Hutchinson and Co., Ltd., 1964), 39.

TRAVEL ABROAD:

Frulovisi's *Peregrinatio*

DRAMATIS PERSONAE

CLERUS adulescens
ARISTOPISTES servus
PORNA meretrix
PROSELITUS senex
ERICHIA mulier
DYNAMIS nutrix
MACROTHYMA mulier
LORARIUS carceris custos
RHYSTES senex
PRESBITES servus
ELPIS ancilla
ANAPAUSIS virgo
‹E›PIICHIS mulier
EVANGELUS adulescens

CHARACTERS

CLERUS, A Young Man
ARISTOPISTES, His Slave
PORNA, A Courtesan
PROSELITUS, An Old Man
ERICHIA, A Woman [Clerus's Mother]
DYNAMIS, A Nurse
MACROTHYMA, A Woman
LORARIUS, A Jailer
RHYSTES, An Old Man [Clerus's Father]
PRESBITES, A Slave
ELPIS, A Servant Girl
ANAPAUSIS, A Young Girl [Rhystes's Stepdaughter]
EPIICHIS, A Woman [Rhystes's Wife and Anapausis's Mother]
EVANGELUS, A Young Man

[*The action takes place in Rhodes, Britain, and Crete*]

ARGUMENTUM

Rhistes Creticus ad
    Britones cum measset,
Nuptiis, quam amabat,
    Erichiam copulat,
Gravidaque facta in patriam
    recta graditur.
Clerus natus, peregre
    patrem qui quaerebat,
Rodi servum amittit simul
    et argentum.
Se quae lactaret dolis, tum
    Clerus decipit,
Et Creten profectus de
    patre recipitur
Icopeta;[1] vir et Anapausis
    Virginis
Ex insperato fit de parente
    cognitus.
Lorarius de servo deceptus
    et delusor simul
Fortunati Cleri cum noverca
    fiunt.

---

[1] *Icopeta*: steward. An illustration of Frulovisi's tendency to use idiosyncratic Latin now and then. The word is defined at the entry for *economicus* in R. E. Latham, *Revised Medieval Latin Word-List from British and Irish Sources* (London: Oxford University Press, 1965), 160.

PLOT

When Rhistes of Crete passed among the Britons, he married Erichia, whom he loved, and yet after getting her with child he went straight back to his homeland. Their son, Clerus, seeking his father abroad at Rhodes, loses both slave and money at the same time. She who entices him with her wiles, Clerus then tricks, and at Crete the father's profit is undertaken by his steward; then the young man unexpectedly meets Anapausis through her father. After the slave deceives Lorarius, he and his deceiver are both set for life, through the stepmother of fortunate Clerus.

PROLOGUS

Si vestri quis quintam quam poeta dedit audisset, ne damnet, nullam quia dixerit se novam daturum.[2] Nunc nec Leo bestia nec crabrones nos insectantur morsibus. Tuti sumus. Non ille se, sed locum dixit cassum fore musis. Nos quintam et ultimam diximus quam illis daret; non principibus nec aliis clausa virtus erit nostri. Iam facta pace cantemus licet, vel si grata fuat magis oratio plana, nullus insectabitur.

Vos, quibus sextam novam primam adducimus, attendite aequis animis,[3] quid sibi velit Peregrinatio nostra. Gratae fuerunt doctis aliae. Nec secus spem concipimus de vobis, quos sapere simul cognoscimus et in bello posse, nec pace minus pollere iusticia.[4] Favete. Silentium iustum implorantibus concedite bonis.

Sin unquam voluptas fuit vestris rebus, nunc immortalitas erit maxima. Nam quid commodi fiat p‹er›egrinantibus, quotque laboribus illorum vita sit et magnis periculis dedita, nobis statim scire poteritis; ubi acta siet P‹er›egrinatio nostra, quam acturi sumus vobis praesentibus. Maius est iter noster quod habuerit. Insolita res est.

Sic et argumentum mutavit.[5] Aliis nam Thessalonicae gesta, Venetiis vel Raven‹n›ae, in Syria seu in Teucris, omnia uno in loco egimus. Veniebant oratores

---

[2] Frulovisi refers to himself in the prologue as both "he" and "we." The former tends to signify his identity as poet, and also himself in the past situation in Venice, while the latter presents the personal and the here-and-now Frulovisi. These distinctions, however, are not fast.

[3] These and similar phrases are virtually formulaic in the prologues of Terence. *Andria* 24: Favete, adeste aequo animo et rem cognoscite. *Eunuch* 44–45: Date operam, cum silentio animum attendite, / ut pernoscatis quid sibi Eunuchus velit. *Phormio* 24: Nunc quid velim animum attendite; 30: Date operam, adeste aequo animo per silentium. *Heauton.* 28: Facite aequi sitis; 35–36: Adeste aequo animo, date potestatem mihi / statariam agere ut liceat per silentium. See also Plautus: *Poenulus* 22: Aequo animo nunc stent; 123: Vos aequo animo noscite. See also the text at note 7 below.

[4] Although throughout the prologue Frulovisi usually employs the second person plural when addressing his audience, these references to war, peace and justice strongly imply a narrower focus on Gloucester personally. Frulovisi hoped for a production of the comedies he wrote in England because at the beginning of both plays he left room in the MS. for the details of a performance. But he was dependent for production on the support of the duke, and this passage demonstrates that fact.

[5] Frulovisi calls attention to his deliberate departure from the unity of place, pointing out in passing that "the custom is the same in Britain."

PROLOGUE

If any of you had attended the fifth play the poet presented, you would know he said he would never write anything else — but don't condemn him for that. For now neither lion-beast nor hornets sting us with their barbs. We are safe. He didn't say the muses had fled from *him*, but from that place. We said the fifth play would be the last he would present to them; but neither by princes nor anyone else will our talent be silenced. Now with calm reestablished, let us sing; or if pleasant dialogue is more pleasing, no one will harry us.

You, to whom we present this distinguished new sixth play, receive with calm minds the meaning of *Travel Abroad*. Learned men enjoyed the other plays. We expect the same reaction from you, whom we know to be both wise and vigorous in war, nor in peace to be less strong for justice. Favor us. Give impartial silence to these good imploring souls.

But if you have ever delighted in your own achievements, now their immortality will be completely assured. For we are about to show you what comforts travelers enjoy as well as how many hardships and great dangers their journeys lead them into; when our *Travel Abroad* is performed for you momentarily. Our hero's journey will be rather extensive. It's an unusual affair.

And so the focus has shifted. Other writers merely describe actions at Thessalonica, Venice or Ravenna, Syria or Troy, but we present all locations in one

vel epistolae legebantur, facta quae narrarent aliis de longinquis locis. Nunc quae Rhodi gesta sunt narrantur Rhodi, quae Cretes Cretes. Similis in Britan‹n›ico mos est. Haec agetur coram: de praesentibus quasi sit acta vobis, cognoscere quod possitis quid ingenium valeat autoris.

Nunc nec maledictis lacessere quaerit alios, nec respondere parat.[6] Favete, adeste aequo animo,[7] ut videatis quid p‹er›egrini nostri apportent novi. Rem gratam dicturi sumus. Ne veremini. Argumentum breve. Ii qui primas partis agent, satis rem claram facient.[8]

---

[6] Terence: *Phormio* 19: Hic respondere voluit, non lacessere.

[7] See note 3 above.

[8] Terence: *Adelphoe* 22–24: dehinc ne expectetis argumentum fabulae: / senes qui primi venient, ei partem aperient, / in agendo partem ostendent.

place. The others use messengers or letters to tell of happenings in distant places. But now when things happen in Rhodes the tale is told at Rhodes, in Crete at Crete. The custom is the same in Britain. Everything happens right here: and when the action takes place, as it were, right in front of you, then you'll know how effective the author's inventiveness is.

He seeks now neither to inflame others with sharp words nor does he prepare to respond. Favor us, be of fair heart, so that you may see what new things our travelers bring. We're about to present a pleasant diversion. Don't worry. The plot is brief. The players in the first scene will make the story clear enough.

Rhodi

Clerus adulescens et Aristopistes servus[9]

CL. Ain tu?

AR. Non dici posset quibus crucibus excruciant adulescentes, spoliant, lacerant.[10]

CL. Malas meretrices!

AR. Pessimas. Ubi vident peregrinum, aream concinnant, rete tendunt. Si sermones inter se conferant, actum est ilico. Captus est misellus.[11] Ve homini! multandus est probe.

CL. Nihil quicquam timeo. Novi ego constantiam et vires meas.[12] Non me vovi Veneri, sed Fortunae.

AR. Cave ne deam commutassis. Pro Fortuna Veneri sacra feras.[13]

---

[9] Frulovisi glosses the head of most scenes with the Greek word from which each character's name is derived, and its meaning in Latin. One of his purposes seems to be displaying his knowledge of Greek, since in the course of the play he explains some of the names more than once. Gloss: ὁ κλῆρος, –ου. *sors* [cleros: a lot used in gambling]. ὁ ἀριστοπιστης, –ου. *vir perfectae fidei* [aristopistes: a man of absolute loyalty].

[10] Terence: *Eunuchus* 382–384: Si in domum meretriciam / deducar et illis crucibus, quae nos nostramque adulescentiam / habent despicatam et quae nos semper omnibus cruciant modis. *Hecyra* 64–65: Et moneo et hortor ne te quoiusquam misereat, / quin spolies mutiles laceres, quemque nacta sis.

[11] Plautus: *Asinaria* 216–218: Auceps quando concinnavit aream, offundit cibum. . . . / semel si sunt captae, rem solvont aucupi.

[12] Wordplay: *Vis, viris* means not only strength of purpose or resolution, but also an intense or overwhelming nature, as of a passionate person; and the force used to obtain sexual gratification. Clerus, callow, surely is unaware.

[13] Wordplay: *venus, veneris* also denotes sexual intercourse. The double entendre here is set up in the preceding speech by Clerus's straightforward use of the word to denote the goddess.

[SCENE I:] RHODES

Young Clerus and his slave Aristopistes

[Enter in conversation]

CL. Are you serious?

AR. I can't tell you the kind of agonies they put young men through, they steal their clothes, they maim their ...

CL. Vicious courtesans!

AR. They're the worst. When they see a traveler, they swarm around the square, they spread their nets. If they plot among themselves, he doesn't have a chance. The poor devil's caught. The man's had it! He'll be well punished.

CL. I'm not afraid of anything. I know my determination and my firmness. I made no vows to Venus, Fortune's the goddess for me.

AR. Be careful you don't switch goddesses. Instead of Fortune, you might just make some sacred offerings to Venus.

CL.   Non fecero. Credin adeo ignavum me quod hos velim de me rumores in
      patriam proferri? "Hem, decus hominis! Clerus penates missos fecit suos,
      ut honorem, gloriam, et rem faciat; et servibit meretricibus."[14] Nusquam
      fiet.

AR.   Modo possis. Quod si queas, nihil melius neque fortius. Verum cave ne
      rete captus pereas. Deus is est, inexpugnatus qui hinc abit. Doctae sunt ad
      perniciem nimis.[15]

CL.   Quid ergo consulis? Pernoctemus hic ruri, ne quum urbem ingressi sumus,
      malam conveniamus?

AR.   Non. Longum esset istud. Ex portu nulla quatriduum solvetur navis. Belli-
      gerant praeterea Rhodi cum Assyriis. In suburbio tuti esse nequimus.

CL.   Quid vis faciam igitur?[16]

AR.   Ingrediamur urbem. Verum male timeo tibi et crumenae.

CL.   Te faciam thesaurum, istuc quod tantopere timeas.

AR.   Sic velim.

CL.   Et tu fac fidelis fuas.

AR.   Hui, etiam mihi non fidem habes? Tot maria legimus, ubi e patria nos
      abiimus, Britan⟨n⟩icum, Superum, Elespontum. Tot terras peragravimus.
      Necdum periculo satis fui.[17]

CL.   Fuisti. Tute mihi metum iniicis de istarum tecnis. Fidem habeo tamen pru-
      dentiae tuae, quod natu grandior sies. Atque audin? Certum istuc est in
      pectore sententiae mihi, peregre mori vel alia gloria redire.

AR.   Ergo vita mulieres.

CL.   Vitaro. Sed quid credis istam bonam fortunam usquam terrarum posse
      comperiri?

AR.   Credo.

CL.   Hem, ubi? Heu male timeo, quanta fuerit frugalitas nostra, ne argentum
      breve sit.

AR.   Ne time. Longum erit.

---

[14] A candid use of *servire* in its sexual meaning. See J. N. Adams, *The Latin Sexual Vocabulary* (Baltimore: Johns Hopkins University Press, 1982), 163–64. See also note 22.

[15] Plautus: *Bacchides* 373: Omnis ad perniciem instructa domus. Terence: *Heauton.* 450: Quam ea nunc
instructa pulchre ad perniciem siet.

[16] Frulovisi here shows the feckless young master dependent on his slave for guidance, a technique
of characterization Terence uses: *Andria* 351–352: Pam. Obsecro te, quam primum hoc me libera miserum metu. Davos. Em, / libero; 384: Pam. Cedo igitur quid faciam, Dave? Davos. Dic te ducturum.
Pam. Hem.

[17] Terence: *Andria* 821: Satis pericli incepi adire.

CL.   That'll never happen. Do you think I'm so shiftless I'd want to have that kind of rumor carried back home about me? "Well, that's Clerus for you! He's thrown off his household gods, and his honor and glory and all else with them. He'll be a slave to his wenches." Nope, that'll never happen.

AR.   I can only hope. But if you could stick to your guns, there'd be nothing better or braver. Really, take care you're not lost, a captive in those nets. He's a god who leaves here unconquered. When it comes to ruination, they know every trick in the book.

CL.   Then what do you advise? Shall we spend the night here in the country, so when we enter the city we don't meet bad luck?

AR.   No, too far away. But not a ship will leave the port for four days. And as if that wasn't enough, Rhodes is at war with the Assyrians, so we wouldn't be safe outside the city.

CL.   Then what do you want me to do?

AR.   Let's go into the city. But I'm really worried about you and your purse.

CL.   If you're so skittish about the place, I'll make you the bank.

AR.   I'd like that.

CL.   Just make sure you stay loyal.

AR.   Well, so now you don't trust me? After all the seas we've crossed since we left home — the Britannic, the Adriatic, the Hellespont. And all the lands we've traveled through. Haven't I been strong enough in tight spots?

CL.   Of course you have. But you've got me scared to death of the wily ways of those women. All the same you're older, so I trust your good sense. Yes, and do you hear? My heart's telling me in no uncertain terms, either we'll die on the road or go back home covered with glory.

AR.   Just make sure you shun those women.

CL.   Consider them shunned. But do you believe such good fortune could be found anywhere else in the world?

AR.   Of course.

CL.   Well, where? Oh, I'm really afraid we haven't watched our pennies enough, and our money will run short.

AR.   Don't worry. It will last.

CL.   Cape igitur.
AR.   Cedo.[18]
CL.   En tibi, et sequere.
AR.   I prae.
CL.   Quam male consulunt sibi, qui certa pro incertis missa faciunt!

       Magnus animus sed parum utilis.

       O mala sitis! Quid mihi venit in mentem aliena quaerere? Quae sero con-
       veniam, conveniam tamen, etsi manus in meas nunc illa quam quaero devo-
       laret.[19]

AR.   Here, nunc haud opus ista consultatione credo. Priusquam agas quicquam,
       consilio et bono consilio; postquam consulueris, tunc facto est opus.[20]
       Praeteritorum non est consultatio.

       Quod tute voluisti, ferendum est aequo animo. Modo vivas honeste, non
       despero quin fortassis talem sortem potiare, ut patriam tuam omnino
       flocifacias. Ignavos et timidos, non fortes, Fortuna laedit; iuvat potius.[21]

---

[18] Rather than *cēdō*, I yield, this is *cedo*, "hand [it] over, give [it] here." The *OLD* entry cites
numerous instances of this word's use by Plautus, as well as several by Terence. In addition, see
Menaechmi 386, where Menaechmus of Syracuse gives his purse to his slave Messenio in front of
Erotium's house; and *Asinaria* 3.3, particularly 654–657, where, with the direction of the cash flow
reversed, the master Argyrippus is trying to get his money back from his slave Leonida.

[19] By picturing the girl flying into his hands, Clerus is reversing the roles in the birding metaphor
Aristopistes used to warn him about the *meretrices*.

[20] Sallust, *Cat.* 1.6: Nam et prius quam incipias consulto et ubi consulueris mature facto opus est.

[21] Terence: *Phormio* 203: Fortis fortuna adiuvat.

CL.   Then take it.

AR.   Give it here.

CL.   [*Clerus gives him the purse*] There, it's all yours — now let's go.

AR.   Lead on.

CL.   How badly people fare who take their own advice, who trade certainties for uncertainties.

[*Looks sidelong at Aristopistes*]

A great soul but not practical enough.

[*One of the courtesans passes by*]

Oo! Evil desire! Why does pursuing something exotic come into my mind? I'm meeting her too late, but I'm still meeting her — even if the girl I want should fly into my arms right now.

AR.   Master, I believe there's hardly a need right now for such thoughts. Before you do anything, take counsel, take good counsel; after you've taken counsel, then it's necessary to take action. There's no counsel for what's already done.

[*Holds up the purse*]

You wanted this yourself. Now bear it with good grace. Live honorably, and I won't worry that you'll perhaps come under the power of some fatal fate, or throw off your homeland and hearthside altogether. Fortune beats down cowards and the fearful, but not the steadfast. Them she helps.

CL.   Benefacis.

       Spem iniicis.

       Pauper esse nequeo, quoad huiuscemodi comitem habuero.
AR.   Facio meum officium quod est, quum servio fideliter.[22] Et tu si quando
       deos propicios habueris, non despero quod boni mihi quippiam erogaveris.
CL.   Ne dubita.
AR.   Bono animo sum ego.

       Sic et te fore velim.
CL.   Quod possum, facio.
AR.   Audacter facias.

---

[22] Wordplay: *servire*, to serve, and *officium*, office or duty, both have sexual connotations of rather
broad range. See Adams, *Latin Sexual Vocabulary*, 163–64. The context here is of a slave from the prov-
inces uttering unintentional sexual innuendo, in a scene where he is exhorting his master to a sweaty-
palmed abstinence. For another instance of such unintended innuendo, see Clerus's speech at note 12.
See also Clerus's use of *servibit* in an intentionally sexual context at note 14 above.

CL.   You advise well.

       [*Aristopistes starts on ahead*]

       You inspire hope.

       [*A courtesan brushes Clerus, lingers*]

       I can't be a poor man as long as I've got a friend like you.

AR.   [*his back to Clerus*] I perform the duty that is mine when I serve you faithfully. And you, if ever the gods do you a favor, I'm not without hope that you'll do one for me.

CL.   [*still with the courtesan*] Trust me.

AR.   Oh, I do.

       [*Turns and sees the two*]

       And I hope you'll return the favor.

CL.   I do the possible.

AR.   May you act boldly.

Clerus adulescens et Porna mulier[23]

CL.   Quid hoc malum infortunii obiectum est mihi? Mitto tam duram peregri-
nationem: et servum habeo quoque, meam qui iuventum excruciat. Semper
mores canit mulierum. Minatur inopiam, animo si morem gero meo. Quid?
Quis credat pecuniam in manu servi? Herum nihil posse? Ni mater me tantopere tot exorasset precibus, nusquam commisissem, servus plus quod ha-
beret in manu quam herus suus. Sed ferendum est.

O pulcras mulieres! Omnis ex animo nostrarum nunc deleo quippe. Quid
facies praedicem? Sapiens est. Me novit profecto. Argentum parvi ducerem,
modo possim amori obsequellam facere. Sed quid haec me sic prospectat
mulier? Medius forma!

POR.   Ἐνωτισάι με, νεανίσκε. Καὶ μὴ ὑπερίδες τὸ προσωπόν μου. Ἡγάπις
σου εἶμι ἐγω.

CL.   Τίνι λέγεις, γ‹υ›νή?[24]

POR.   Σοῖ.

---

[23] [gloss:] ἡ, πόρνη, -ης *meretrix* [porne: public prostitute, harlot].

[24] Shown as γηνή in both Previté-Orton, *Opera* and St. John's College MS. 60.

[SCENE 2: RHODES]

Clerus the young man and a woman, Porna

CL. Why does Lady Luck have it in for me? I'm making this hard journey, and on top of that I've got a slave who torments my youth. He's always harping on the morals of women. He says if I put my thoughts into action, we'll end up with nothing. Who'd believe it? Who'd put their money in the hands of a slave? Can't the master do anything? If my mother hadn't begged me so much to always do what he said, I'd never have turned it over, and now the slave has it all and I've got nothing. Well, that's how it is right now.

[*Some of the courtesans cross the stage*]

O, beautiful women! Now I'm definitely wiping every one of you right out of my mind. Should I guess what you're up to? He's wise, he really knows me. Money wouldn't mean a thing if I could scratch this itch. But why is this woman looking me over? What a figure!

POR. Listen to me, young man. Don't despise my face. I'm your lover.

CL. Who are you talking to, woman?

POR. You.

CL.   Peregrinus sum nec loquellam bene novi. Quis e Britan‹n›ico Graecum doc-
tum venit?[25] Mulier, si linguam mutassis, hic verba commutabimus inter
nos. Sin aliter, vale. 'Ελίνος οὐκ εἰμι.

POR.   Latinus?

CL.   Non, sed loquellam bene novi.

POR.   Γινώσκεις?

CL.   Nescio quid dicas.

POR.   Dico an Latinum noveris.

CL.   Novi, et scio.

POR.   Quid tibi rhodu‹s› videtur?

CL.   Minoris quam facies tua.

POR.   Gratias ago tibi, mi patrone. Sed quid? Vin mecum mane prandium esse?

CL.   Non. Modo servum parare iussi apud hospitem meum. Alias venero.[26]
Nunc vale. Iam fabricat in me dolos. Quid ego invitus hodie feci boni,
quum argent‹um› servo tradidi? Hui, timendum erat illi crumenae. Profecto
verum est quod aiunt: "Argentum auferas adulescenti simul et venerem."
Religio est istanc adire quod obulo cassus siem.[27] At servassem saltem
minam!

POR.   Quid tute tecum?

---

[25] A true remark at the time, although expressed with more forthrightness than prudence since
Humphrey was the prime mover in trying to bring Greek studies to England in the first half of the
fifteenth century. See George R. Stephens, *The Knowledge of Greek in England in the Middle Ages* (Ph.D. diss.,
University of Pennsylvania, 1933; repr. Folcroft, PA: Folcroft Library Editions, 1979), 100–2. Indeed
Humphrey's efforts were merely the beginnings of a movement that would culminate only in the next
century with the generation of Grocyn, Colet, Linacre and More. See Grady Smith, "Books and the Development of English Humanism," *Fifteenth-Century Studies* 6 (1983): 232–43.

[26] Literally, "I shall have come at another time," this sentence contains several plays on words, some
of them double entendres. *Venire*, to come, is not the equivalent of the English in the sense of experienc-
ing orgasm. However, *pervenire*, to arrive, does have this meaning and is indirectly evoked here. Moreover,
venero resonates with *venus*, *veneris* which denotes both the goddess of love and the sexual act; in addition
it also signifies the best throw in dicing with *tali*, and so relates, at a remove, to the etymology of
Clerus's name. *Venus* and *Fortuna* are simultaneously evoked. Finally, the adverb *alias*, "at another time,"
has the same form as the feminine accusative plural of the adjective meaning *other*. Although *venio* is in-
transitive, license permits the omission of a preposition such as *ad*, thus allowing the reading, "I shall
have come to other women." For the sexual aspects of this wordplay see Adams, *Latin Sexual Vocabulary*,
144. See also note 22.

[27] *Siem*, the pre-Ciceronian form of the present subjunctive of *sum*, is frequently found in both Plautus and Terence. The present subjunctive in this causal clause indicates that the reason given is on the
authority of another. Clerus blames his situation on Aristopistes, assuming thereby a certain subservience
in their relationship. Terence: *Heauton.* 228: Tum quod dem ei "recte" est; nam nil esse mihi religiost
dicere.

CL. I'm a traveler and I don't understand the language well. Who comes from Britain knowing Greek? Woman, if you change languages we can talk together. If not, farewell. I'm not Greek.

POR. Are you from Latium?

CL. No, but I understand the language well.

POR. Do you understand?

CL. I don't understand what you're saying.

POR. I'm asking whether you know Latin.

CL. I know it, and understand it, too.

POR. How do you like Rhodes?

CL. Not as much as that face of yours.

POR. Thank you, my patron. But what now? Would you like to join me in the wee hours for a little bite?

CL. No. I've just sent my slave to prepare lunch at my lodgings. Some other time and I'll come. Now goodbye. [*aside:*] Already she lays traps for me. What good did I do today, without knowing it, when I gave the money to my slave? Well, he had to be afraid for that purse. It's really true what they say: "You'd take away a young man's silver along with his love." I'm obeying my "thou shalt not" because I'm flat broke. But if only I'd saved a little loose change!

POR. What do you have in mind?

CL.   Doleo mihi negocium esse. Danda est opera rei. Mercatorem expecto, merces qui comparet meas. Alias venero.[28]

POR. Nihil facis, aedepol. Mercatores te bene conquirent. Nemini offeras merces tuas, cui care ven‹du›ndas.[29]

Oblata non possunt esse cara.[30]

CL.   Vera loquitur. Istaec cara nusquam esset.

Sed nihil est carius tamen quam quod emi non potest.

POR. Adulescens, qui vocare?

CL.   Clerus.

POR. Clere, me forsitan ex aliquarum ingenio iudicas, quae impudicae vitam degunt? Ego quanquam hospes ad me peregrinos saepius receptem meae domi, tamen nusquam avara fui, quod aurum pluris faciam quam egregium virum. Ego, ut sententiam meam noscas, hic apud me, si voles, diverticulum fecero tibi. Nec ullum est statutum precium. Ubi liberalitatem meam bene noveris, si quid dederis, non precium sed munus illud ego fecero. Iam biennium effigiem non vidi talem, qualis in te sita est. Cupio nimis in familiaritatem tuam recipi.

CL.   Id mutuum facis, et me polliceor facturum. Verum mane non possum esse tecum. Servum convenero.[31] Quid istac super re dederit consilii, id exsequar.

POR. Per dium fidium non abibis.

---

[28] The repetition of *Alias venero* gives opportunity to express a more connotative meaning. See note 26 above. Plautus expresses this same kind of double entendre at *Truculentus* 547: Mox huc cubitum venero.

[29] *Venuendas* in Frulovisi's manuscript; Previté-Orton flags it with a (*sic*). Plautus uses the form to which I have corrected the word three times: *Amphitryon* 2 (*vendundisque*), *Mostellaria* 279 (*vendundust*), and *Poenulus* 1018 (*vendundas*).

[30] Double entendre. Porna shifts her meaning from Clerus's merchandise to her own. Hers, she tells Clerus, won't be expensive. Callow, he agrees in the next line that his own wares are of little value, implying in the context of her double meaning, which has gone completely over his head, that her merchandise is not worth much.

[31] Literally, "I am meeting my slave." *Convenio* in late Latin prose was a synonym for *coitus*. See Adams, *Latin Sexual Vocabulary*, 179.

CL. Too bad I'm so busy, but business before pleasure. I'm waiting for a merchant to close on my merchandise. Some other time for Venus.

POR. You're doing nothing of the sort, by Pollux. Merchants are seeking you to
advantage? You're not offering anyone your goods, but you'd sell to them
at a premium price.

[*double entendre:*]

But what's for sale can't be all that expensive.

CL. You're right. It's pretty cheap stuff.

[*Porna reacts as he looks her over*]

But nothing's dearer than what can't be bought.

POR. Young man, your name?

CL. Clerus.

POR. Clerus, perhaps you're judging me from the character of other women, who
live life loosely? I may receive travelers as guests in my home — yes, rather
frequently. But I was never so greedy that I made gold more important
than a strong, upstanding man. So you'll know what I have in mind, I'll
arrange a diversion for you, if you want, here by me. And nothing has a
fixed price on it. Once you're intimately acquainted with my generosity
and want to give me anything, I won't think of it as a fee but a gift. I
haven't seen a man quite like you in two years now. And I want so much
to be your dear, close friend.

CL. You make the feeling mutual — and I swear it will happen. Oh, but look
— I *can't* be with you this morning. I'm hooking up with my slave. What
he advises about business, well, that's it.

POR. [*Putting some moves on him*] By divine Jupiter, you will not go.

CL.   Iam me tenet. Sed stultus sum. Quid faciet illa mihi, cum servus argentum
       habeat omne? Edendum est apud istanc. Vestem hanc non detrahet ipsa
       mihi. Damnum nullum hic: lucrum esse potest. Tantum inest mali, quod
       bonus ille servus in fame fuerit.[32] Montes huic ego pollicebor auri.[33]
       Non primum solutio fiet.

       Servum, quod est, dicam argentum habere.
POR.   Iam enumerasti rationes tuas?
CL.   Facerem quod velles, si servus hic adesset, qui nobis vinum saltem afferret.
POR.   Istic vino grana terunt.
CL.   Qui?
POR.   Ut apud vos aqua, sic istic vino molas verrunt. Magna est hic rerum om-
       nium vilitas. Ingredere,[34] sodes.
CL.   Faciendum est.[35]
POR.   Merito te amo.
CL.   Quid mihi faciet? In portu navis mea sita est, ubi tempestas nulla. Tibi,
       non mihi, dolos facis.
POR.   Ingressus est. O sapientem virum! Solon, si videas, videtur. In area nunc es-
       cam edes haud ab re aucupis.[36]

       Tractabo te ex sententia.

       Ingredior ego quoque, ut lactem nebulonem.[37]

---

[32] *In fame*, "in hunger," evokes *infame*, "deserving of ill repute," a nicely ironic juxtaposition with
bonus ille servus.

[33] Terence: *Phormio* 67–68: Is senem per epistulas / pellexit, modo non montis auri pollicens.

[34] Double entendre. "Sometimes verbs meaning 'go in' are used elliptically in the sense 'go in (to
a room, *coeundi causa*)'." Adams, *Latin Sexual Vocabulary*, 176.

[35] Literally, "it must be done." Frulovisi has established the passive periphrastic as a verbal aspect
of Clerus's character. Now, used here in the context of adolescent sexual urgency, this "roundabout way
of speaking" is incongruous and funny.

[36] Plautus uses the birding metaphor even more elaborately: *Asinaria* 219–220: Aedes nobis area est,
auceps sum ego, / esca est meretrix, lectus inlex est, amatores aves. See also *Menaechmi* 338–345, where
in a similar scene Messenio warns Menaechmus of Syracuse about the methods courtesans use to snare
their patrons.

[37] *Tracto* commonly signifies both caressing and masturbation. The verbal noun *tractatio* describes the
actions of the male in intercourse. Compounds (*contrecto, attrecto, pertracto*) take meanings into even more
varied areas. See Adams, *Latin Sexual Vocabulary*, 186–87. *Lacto* here means to lead on, to entice, but
strongly evokes *lacteo*, to be full of milk or juice. The reverberations between *tractabo* and *lactem* produce
a graphically suggestive effect.

CL. [*aside:*] She's got me now. But I'm a fool. What will she do for me when
     the slave's got all the money? Well, I'll eat at her house, but she won't
     coax me out of these clothes. No loss here: it could be an advantage. And
     while I eat, too bad — that upright slave will go hungry. I'll promise her
     mountains of gold, but say I can't pay up front because …

     [*searching for a plausible lie*]

     I'll say my slave has all the money. No, wait — that's the truth.

POR. Have you finished your calculations?

CL. I'd do as you wish if my slave were here, he'd at least bring wine to us.

POR. They often use wine to grind the grain hereabouts.

CL. What?

POR. You drive the millstone with water, but here they use wine because it's
     worth so little. Come in now, if you want.

CL. Oh, I want, I want.

POR. I was meant to love you.

CL. [*aside:*] What will she do for me on credit? The weather's fine, but my ship
     can't leave port. You're cheating yourself, not me. [*exits*]

POR. He's gone in. Oh, a wise man! A Solon, or so he seems, to look at him.
     But now in the town square you're taking the bait, much to the bird-
     catcher's advantage.

     [*Clerus leans out the door*]

     I'll handle things any way you want.

     [*Clerus says "ooh" and exits*]

     Now I go in, too, to milk this hell-raiser.

RHODI

Proselitus senex et Clerus adulescens[38]

PRO. Nequeo satis mirari unde cupiditas haec stulta mortalibus vigeat, in aliena
pergere: cum lupus sit homo homini, si peregrinus fuat.[39] Ita mihi dii
deaeque faveant omnes, uti nusquam memini tam f‹o›eda, sic iniusta fieri.
Heu, quum recordor, nequeo quin lacrimem miser. Quot quantisque in-
commoditatibus vitam subiicit, alios qui fines ingreditur!

CL. Quid dicet modo? Iam non me suppilabunt. Hem, una sensit, meae quid
vires valeant. Hoc unum est quod reputo palmarium. Dolos, perniciem
com‹m›unem peregrinorum, meretricum tecnas, labes vici. Quae me de-
ceptum parata venerat decepi.[40]

PRO. In carnuficinam ducitur adulescens mehercle non ingenuus.

CL. Quae me spoliare pararat, spoliavi.

PRO. Quem audio spoliasse istunc? Adulescens est. Peregrinus est. Hui, male timeo huic quoque. Accedam. Compellabo virum.

CL. In viginti dies satis fuerit haec praeda.

PRO. Adulescens, quisquis vocare, respice ad me.

CL. Clerus. Pater, qui vis? Iube, tibique statim audiens dicto fuero.

---

[38] Gloss: ὁ προσέλιτος, -ου. *advena* [proselitos: stranger, foreigner].

[39] Plautus: *Asinaria* 495: Lupus est homo homini, non homo, quom qualis sit non novit.

[40] Double entendre: *venerat*, the pluperfect of *venio*, is also the present tense of *venero*, one of the
meanings of which is to engage in sex. In addition see Terence, *Eunuchus* 382–387: Chaerea *adulescens* tells
his slave Parmeno that if he tried to swindle his father he would be blamed by the world, but to trick
meretrices would earn him praise from everyone.

[SCENE 3:] RHODES

Old Proselitus and Clerus the Young Man

PRO. [*Alone*] I've never been able to figure it out — this insane need in people to travel abroad in foreign lands. Especially since man's a wolf to a man who's traveling. So the gods and goddesses should look out for me, but I don't remember anything so horrible, such injustice being done. Ah, when I look back, it makes me sad enough to cry over it. When you go to other countries, life is subjected to one indignity after another!

CL. [*Enters dressed in Porna's costume*] Oh, what she'll say. But she won't fleece me now. Right now a certain lady's realizing how unbending are men's strong points. This one really takes the cake — I've beaten those nets, the universal doom of travelers, those courtesans' tricks, that ruination. She came ready to fleece me, and I fleeced her.

PRO. That young man who's being led to the hangman — by Hercules, he's a foreigner.

CL. She was ready to rob me, and I turned the tables on her. [*Produces bag of coins*]

PRO. Do I hear that fellow has robbed someone? He's a young man, a traveler. He's got me scared, too, but I'll go over and speak to the man.

CL. [*Hefting the bag*] This loot should be enough to last twenty days.

PRO. Young man, what's your name? Look at me.

CL. Clerus. Good old sir, what's your wish? Tell me, and no sooner said than done.

PRO. Tantum est quod afferunt alienae terrae: mansuetudinis multum. Cuiatis es?
CL. Gallus.
PRO. Quid te praedae nunc dicere audivi?
CL. Ahahe. Non possum prae risu verba facere.
PRO. Quid est?
CL. Hodie hunc locum adii. Servus meus metum non destitit iniicere de huius-
modi mulieribus: quid doli struant, fallaciae, deceptionis adulescentulis.
Quid multa loquor? Tantum effecit suis verbis, ut bonorum meorum illum
statim thesaurum fecerim. Ubi ad hospitem pergit, ilico parata est quae me
spoliare credat. Quid opus est verbis? Obsonium dedit insuper et pallam:
quam contexi faciam aureis litteris, pollicitus sum. Et in aurum hanc con-
vertam totam. Quaerebam servum, cui nunc ostenderem quid in me salis
sedeat. Fallunt nebulones.
PRO. Tute tibi sapiens videris. Sed ad ludum sin allectaberis, rem omnem solves
hospiti. Misereor ego tui, qui locum nescias ist‹a›ec ubi dicas. Ego pol te
monitum velim, ut fugias mulieres simul et Rhodios. Non dici potest quo
studio suas tueantur. Tantisper gaudeas licet, dum se deceptam nesciat.[41]
Ubi res‹c›iscat, tu peribis.
CL. Hem, quid ais?
PRO. Sic res est ut audis. Sed accipe quid hodie miseri viderim.
CL. Quid?
PRO. Malos Graecos. Adulescens aedepol liberalis pro exule vinctus, ut latro
ducebatur. Accessi, causam ut discerem infortunii sui. Negabat homo, sanc-
teque iurabat patriam istam, ni qua ducebatur hora, vidisse nunquam. Hominem, quum videas, quanti vis precii esse videtur. Tristis severitas in
vultu. Atticam vere dicas illius eloquentiam.

---

[41] Plautus: *Menaechmi* 193: Meretrix tantisper blanditu, dum illud quod rapiat videt.

PRO. So wonderful what other countries offer: much respect. Your nationality?

CL. French.

PRO. And what was this loot I heard you speaking of just now?

CL. Oh — ha ha. I can't talk from laughing.

PRO. What's going on?

CL. I arrived at this place today. My slave never stopped harping on women of a certain kind, because they set traps and snares and scams for young men. What more's to say? His words made such an impression on me that right there and then I made him keeper of my cash. Then as soon as he left for the inn, a woman showed up here, planning to rob me. Any more words needed? She gave me food and a robe, and — and what I've glossed over I'll turn into glittering prose, I promise. I'll turn this whole affair into gold. I was looking for my slave, I should show him now what wit there is in me. They cheat good-for-nothings.

PRO. You seem a bit wiser already. But if you needed a little amusement, you could have taken care of the whole business at your inn. I sympathize with you when you start talking about a place you don't know. By Pollux, I wish you'd been warned to stay away from all the Rhodians as well as the women. I can't tell you how closely they watch out for each other. She lets you enjoy yourself just as long as she doesn't know she's been tricked herself. But when she finds out, you'll be lost.

CL. What do you advise?

PRO. Here's how the matter stands right now. But you've got to say yes to what even now seems a heavy burden to me.

CL. What?

PRO. These wretched Greeks. By Pollux, a free young man — treated like an exile, like a thief. I come over to find out the cause of his misfortune. And here's this fellow denying, and swearing by his very homeland no less, that he hadn't seen a thing, during a certain hour that he hadn't spent ... that he hadn't spent. When you see the man, he seems upright enough of character. But a melancholy gravity mars his face. Truly you should speak of him with Attic eloquence.

[*Aristopistes enters chained, guarded by Lorarius*]

CL.   Hei mihi! Malum divinat animus.

PRO.   Quid?
CL.   Hunc esse servum meum.
PRO.   Bono animo sis. Facie ille erat liberali.

CL.   Hem, ah, oh! Expedi! Me enecas.

        Quid? Illi erat argentum in manu?
PRO.   Nihil quicquam. Sed rem suam, quae minus sua foret deplorabat. Erichiam
        invocabat saepe.
CL.   Ea mihi mater fuit. Is est servus meus, me qui plus amat oculis suis.[42] Il-
        lius nomen nunquid meministi?
PRO.   Pulcre. Aristopistem se dicebat; illi vero minime sed Licum esse.[43] Vinc-
        tus erat manicis ferreis. Nec solum illum dicebant, qui socium habuisset
        facinoris.
CL.   Perii miser. Nonquid orabo causam servi pecuniaeque meae?
PRO.   Nescio. Avari sunt Graeci nimis. Periculum et tibi fuerit, ne perdant argen-
        tum. Ego tibi, ut abeas, nescio satis suadere. Quum abfueris, tute per pa-
        tronos causam tuam ages. Siquid ego possum, non aliud agam pro te quam
        pro unico gnato meo. Num quid me vis?
CL.   Ut mihi consulas, quid agi censeas.[44]
PRO.   Dixi, ut abeas. Satius est argentum et servum quam vitam perdere.[45]
CL.   Quo id pacto fiet, cui nihil in manu siet?
PRO.   Habes hanc pallam.
CL.   Habeo. Quid tum postea?
PRO.   Vendas.

---

[42] Terence: *Adelphoe* 701: Ni magis te quam oculos nunc amo meos; 903: Qui te amat plus quam
hosce oculos.

[43] Literally, "He called himself Aristopistes; but he's by no means a [?] Lichas. He was chained with
iron manacles." Perhaps Frulovisi intends Lichas, the attendant of Hercules who brought him the fatal
robe. In his death agony Hercules blamed Lichas. When he tossed his servant into the air, the man
turned to stone and sank into the sea.

[44] Plautus: *Amphitryon* 1128–1129: Ego Teresiam coniectorem advocabo et consulam / quid faciundum censeat. *Poenulus* 794–795: Nunc ibo, amicos consulam, quo me modo / suspendere aequom censeant potissimum.

[45] Terence: *Adelphoe* 234–235: Ut sit satius perdere / quam aut nunc manere tam diu aut tum
persequi.

CL.   Oh, no! I smell trouble.

[*Tries to hide because of his costume*]

PRO.   What?

CL.   That's my slave.

PRO.   Don't panic. He's got a free man's face.

[*Goes over to eavesdrop on Lorarius and Aristopistes*]

CL.   Oh gods! Free *me*. You're killing me.

[*Proselitus returns*]

Well? Did he have money in his hand?

PRO.   Nothing at all. But he kept wailing about his situation, which apparently is less his own. He kept calling out 'Erichea'.

CL.   That's my mother. He's my slave, all right, who loves me more than his own eyes. Do you remember his name?

PRO.   Clearly. He called himself Aristopistes. Well, he won't be skipping across the sea very soon. He was chained with iron manacles. And they spoke not only of him, but someone he's in cahoots with.

CL.   Oh, no, that's me. How do I plead my case so I get back my slave and my money?

PRO.   I don't know. These Greeks are really greedy. It will get dangerous for you, if they should 'lose' the money. I don't know how to urge you strongly enough to leave. After you've gone, you can safely argue your case through lawyers. And if I can, I'll help you like I'd help an only son of mine. Now, what do you need from me?

CL.   Your best advice. What should I do?

PRO.   What I said, leave here. It's better to lose both money and slave than to lose your life.

CL.   But how can I leave empty-handed?

PRO.   You have this outfit.

CL.   Do I ever. But what good is it?

PRO.   Sell it.

CL.   Cui? Me furem dicent, interii, quum ostendero.

PRO.   Mihi vendas. Navem conductam et oneratam habeo. Eam ego deueham
       Thessalonicam in patriam ad meam speratam. Quanti illam facis?

CL.   Quanti gratum est animo tuo.

PRO.   Quattuor minae satis sunt pro re tua.

CL.   Tibi gratias habeo.

PRO.   En accipe. Cretensis nunc e portu celox solvetur. Illam ingredi poteris.

CL.   Me tibi commendo. Tu es patronus, tu magister, tu pater, tuus ego sum
       totus.[46]

PRO.   Fili, mille telis Fortunae subiecta est vita mortalium. Modo saevam, modo
       se blandam ostendit. Hunc premit, hunc in caelum locat. Quem in caelo
       videras, in infernum brevi deiectum audies. Demens est qui utrique vel alte-
       ri fortunae credit.[47] Ne despera. Rem perdidisti. Alibi maiorem facies.
       Cui est virtus, perire nequit.[48]

CL.   Hei misero mihi! In quod me et illum conieci malum, dum incerta pro cer-
       tis quaero.[49] Quid faciam modo? Sin illum relinquo, fidem fallo: qui iura-
       verim mortem me pro meo Aristopiste flocifacturum.[50] Sin illum defendo,
       vitae meae timeo.

PRO.   Quid facias? Illi quando nihil potes, tibi prospectes decet. Auri dira sitis
       est istorum. Fuge, si me amas.

CL.   Fecero.

---

[46] Plautus: *Captivi* 444–445: Tu mihi erus nunc es, tu patronus, tu pater, / tibi commendo spes
opesque meas. Former teacher Frulovisi adds *magister* to the list of titles demanding reverence and obedi-
ence. Terence: *Adelphoe* 455–456: In te spes omnis, Hegio, nobis sitast: / Te solum habemus, tu es patronus, tu pater.

[47] This passage evokes Boethius, *Cons. Phil.* 2 pr. 1.

[48] Plautus: *Amphitryon* 652–653: Virtus omnia in sese habet, omnia adsunt / bona quem penest
virtus.

[49] Plautus: *Pseudolus* 685: Certa mittimus, dum incerta petimus. *Asinaria* 463–466: Credam fore, dum
quidem ipse in manu [argentum] habebo. / Peregrinus ego sum. Sauream non novi. . . . / Ego certe me
incerto scio hoc daturum nemini homini.

[50] Clerus's expression of loyalty to his slave is matched by Aristopistes in his speech opening scene
11. This mutual loyalty evokes the relationship of Philocrates and Tyndarus, master and slave in *Captivi*,
and constitutes an instance of *imitatio*.

CL.   Who'd buy it? They'll call me a thief, when I show up like this.

PRO. Sell it to me. I've chartered a ship and she's all loaded. I can't wait to sail for home and my waiting wife. What can you give for your passage?

CL.   All the thanks I can muster for your generosity.

PRO. Four minae are enough for your situation.

CL.   I thank you.

PRO. Come, agree. My fast Cretan ship will cast off from port any moment now. You can board her.

CL.   I'm in your hands. You're my patron, my teacher, my father, all I am is yours.

PRO. Son, listen now. Our lives are the targets of Fortune, and she's got a thousand arrows. Sometimes she's savage, other times she's charming. Here she throws you down, there she flings you high in the sky. One moment you'll see people up in heaven, the next you'll hear them falling into hell. It's senseless to trust either one side of Fortune or the other. Don't give up hope. You've lost out in this situation. But next time you'll do better. A good man never loses.

CL.   Oh, I'm a walking disaster! This rotten business happened to him and me because I'm seeking out uncertainties instead of certainties. But now what? If I leave him, I'm selling him out: and I promised to stick by my Aristopistes to the death. But if I mount a defense, I could wind up at the end of a rope.

PRO. What can you do? It's right for you to look to the future when there's nothing you can do for him. They've got a fearful thirst for money. Please — leave this place.

CL.   All right. [*Exits*]

PRO. Non audiunt isti verba nostra, qui plura sapimus, quod plura viderimus. Quodcunque audacissimum est, id consilium placet. Miseret me istorum, cum quod errores noverim istius aetatis, tum quod peregrinus ego sum quoque. Quanquam Galli sint et ego Teucer, peregrini tamen sumus omnes. Si non amamur inter nos, in malam crucem[51] eamus necesse fuerit. Sed alia sunt negocia mihi, cui e propinquo navigandum siet. Pergam quo coeperam hoc iter.[52]

---

[51] The phrase *malam crucem* is well represented in Plautus and Terence. See for example *Captivi* 469, *Casina* 641, *Poenulus* 347, *Pseudolus* 335, *Rudens* 176; *Phormio* 368.

[52] Proselitus's willingness to help Clerus, a stranger, calls to mind a recurring Terentian theme, his "larger concern with human relations in general. Some commentators have felt, in fact, that Terence's interest is in the nature of a philosophical position, that man should practice *humanitas*, or 'humaneness,' toward one another." Walter E. Forehand, *Terence* (Boston: Twayne Publishers, 1985), 125.

PRO. Those two, they don't want to hear what I've got to say — but I know a lot because I've seen a lot. Some bold scheme, that's the advice that would please them. They make me sad, because I've not only shared the faults of youth in my day, but I'm a traveler now just like they are. Though they're French and I'm German, we're all travelers. If we don't stick together, we'll all have to cross hell barefoot. But I've got other business to attend to, and soon I have to set sail. I have to get on with this journey I've started.

In Britan‹n›ia

Erichia Mulier et Dynamis Nutrix[53]

ER. Nequeo, mea nutrix. Mortem video, Stiga, manes. O infelicem me! O invenustam![54] Primum virum duxi, qui sic circumduxit; qui paucos mensis redire dixerat, at nusquam venit. Si excessisset e vita, modo meas istud ad
auris devenisset, levius illud fuerat quippe. Vivat necne, id Orcus sciat licet.
Natus est filius, qui molestias levaret mihi. Mores in paternos et is evasit,
vadit, et nescit quo. Me miseram! At saltem sciret paternam patriam,
patrem fortassis conveniret.

DI. Quid tu non illam filio dixti?

ER. Aedepol mansurum credidi si nesciret, et falsa fui. Nunc autem quum memini, quos mihi pater labores decantabat, quae, quot, quantaque pericula
peregrinationibus conveniant, horreo prae formidine; membra metu debilia
fiunt.[55] Patrem amavi, qui meo potitus est flore, magisque dilexi, magis
expetivi, quod ab oculis hinc abesset. Quum natum videbam, Ristem contui
videbar. Hem, desolata sum. Oh sola relicta, miseram mortem video. Non
possum amplius.

DI. Te quando fortunatam credidi et felicem. Sed magnus me tenebat error,
grandis caecitas. Non auro sed animo mortalium divitiae metiendae sunt.

---

[53] Gloss: ἡ ἐρικία, -ας [erikia: quarrel, irritate]. et ὁ πλοῦτος, -ου. id est divitiae: arum [ploutos: that is riches, wealth] et ἡ δύναμις, -εως, fortitudo [dynamis: virtue, strength].

[54] Terence: *Andria* 245: Adeon hominem esse invenustum aut infelicem quemquam ut ego sum.

[55] Plautus: *Casina* 622: Cor metu mortuomst, membra miserae tremunt. *Rudens* 685–686: Miserae quom venit in mentem / mihi mortis, metus membra occupat. Terence: *Adelphoe* 612: Membra metu debilia sunt.

[SCENE 4:] IN BRITAIN

Erichea the Woman [Clerus's Mother] and Dynamis the Nurse

ER. I can't, dear Nurse. I see death, the River Styx, the shades of those gone before. Oh, I've been so unhappy, unhappy in love. I took the first man I saw, he wrapped me around his little finger. He told me he'd come back in a few months, but he never did. If he'd given up the ghost, I'd have heard somehow, and it would be easier to bear. Well, the god of the underworld knows if he lives. The son I bore should bear my troubles for me now. But he's his father's son, too, and he's made his escape. He's rushing off to he doesn't know where. Any wonder I'm so miserable? But if he knew his father's country he might just find him.

DY. But you haven't told the boy his country, have you?

ER. I swear I thought he'd stay home if he didn't know, but I was wrong. And now when I remember his father, reeling off the hardships, all the many great dangers crossing the path of travelers, I'm petrified, my hands tremble with fear. I loved his father, he was my first and only love, and I desired more, sought more, but he went from my eyes. When I saw the baby, it was like looking at his father Rhystes. Now I'm desolate and alone, I see an unhappy death, I can't fight it any more.

DY. I thought you were so fortunate and happy. But I was so mistaken, what a great blindness. Gold isn't the measure of human wealth — that's done with the heart.

ER.   Felicem me quam minus est aequum credere? Summa O inopia nata forem
       et viro desponsata, viro quicum aetatem vixissem. Quid beatitudinis esse
       potest mulieri, a viro si separata sit? At non gustassem saltem quae sit viri
       voluptas, minus ego cruciarer, crede, Dinami.

DI.   Credo. Neque gratus filii fuit discessus animo meo. Num hunc lacte nutri-
       vi? Amavi pro meo? Me coluit semper? Sed iacturam nostram fortiter fera-
       mus. Clerum etiam visuras nos non despero. Veniet et illius fors pater. Eri-
       chia, ne te crucia, anime mi.

ER.   Non possum aliter esse. Devolat anima profecto. Tene me. O Clere, Clere,
       parricida peregre in alienas terras graderis.

DI.   Ah, istuc ne dixeris. Istuc dii prohibeant. Ingrediamur, Erichia mea. Paula-
       tim animam recipe. Natum et virum etiam videbis.

ER.   Ingrediamur. Ad Acheronta videbo. Tene me. Decido.

DI.   Quanquam sexus istud nobis afferat labilitatis, animo bono fac sies et con-
       stanti. Tunc nullus in te praevalebit morbus.

ER.   Didicimus istuc semper ⟨a⟩egris facere, sed in me inducere nequeo. Ohoh!

DI.   Respira. Te subducam. Dies aegritudines minuunt homini.[56]

ER.   Ohoh!

DI.   Hyperiphania, Mechia, omnes ancillae, huc descendite! Heram comprendite!

Quanta mortalibus caecitas iniecta est ob suas divitias! Est quis dives? Reli-
quos statim mortalium spernit, deos nihili facit, se putat immortalem. At
est deus,[57] qui omnia quae fiunt videt et audit, pauperum et vindex debi-
lium. Is statim moerores contra parat.

---

[56] Terence: *Heauton.* 421–422: Audio / dici, diem adimere aegritudinem hominibus.

[57] A curious departure from the otherwise polytheistic world of *Peregrinatio*. Perhaps Frulovisi intended the *deus* of this speech to be insurance against the kind of charges that resulted from including
pagan deities in his second comedy, *Claudi Duo*. See the introduction at note 12, which shows Frulovisi
shading his use of Ciceronian borrowings for the *De Republica* toward monotheistic orthodoxy.

ER. Who'd believe how little happiness I have now? Oh, I was born totally helpless, promised to a man I should have spent a lifetime with. What happiness can there be for a woman if she lives apart from her husband? If I simply hadn't known the pleasure of a man, Dynamis, I wouldn't be so miserable, believe me.

DY. I do. Nor was the boy's departure welcome to my heart. Didn't I nurse him with my milk? Didn't I love him like my own? And didn't he always honor me? But let's bear that loss with courage. I'm not without hope that we'll see Clerus, too. He'll come and maybe his father, too. Erichea, dear friend, don't torture yourself.

ER. I can't be something I'm not. My soul's almost ready to go. Hold me. O Clerus, Clerus, you kill your mother though you're traveling in foreign lands.

DY. Ah, don't say that. May the gods prevent that. Let's go in, Erichia. Ease your heart a little. You'll see your boy and your husband, too.

ER. Yes, let's go in. I'll see that river soon. Hold me, I'm slipping.

DY. Though our sex makes us frail, keep your heart good and constant. Then no distress will get the upper hand in you.

ER. I could always make the sickness of others go away, but I can't do it for myself. Oh, oh!

DY. Breathe. I'll support you. Time heals all our wounds.

ER. Oh, oh!

DY. Hyperiphania, Mechia, maidservants all, come down here! Take hold of the mistress!

[*The maidservants help Erichea off*]

How great the blindness thrust upon mortals because of their wealth! Who's really rich? One who constantly ignores the rest of humanity, treats the gods like dirt, thinks he'll live forever? But God's over all, He sees and hears everything that's done, he's the protector of the poor and helpless. He's constantly providing against sorrows.

Haec mulier, adulescentula quamvis, quia potens auro, caeteros spernebat. Deus autem cupidinem imposuit illi Cretensis hominis, qui uxores duceret. Duxit illam uxorem, obsequitur animo. Verum quamdiu? Solos tris mensis. Abiit bonus ille vir. Gravidam tamen puero fecerat. Nascitur novus Cretensis matris magno malo. Nam nec virum alterum ducere potuit, et desponsata vidua vixit. Puer patrem quaerit; mater negare. Postquam est vir factus, illum quaesitum abiit. O mortalium pecuniam! O divitias vestras, quas nisi noveritis, beati vivetis! Ingredior et ego, non quod sic amicer mulieri sed Clero, quem lacte laboribusque nutrivi meis.

[*deeply concerned*]

When she was young, this woman turned her back on others because of the power of money. But God filled her with desire for that man from Crete — collecting wives, that Cretan. He married this woman because she obeyed her heart. And how long did it last? Three months, thank you, and then that good man left. But he'd gotten her pregnant with the boy. A new child of Crete was born to a mother in great pain. For she couldn't marry another man, you see, so she lived like a widow. The boy asks about his father, the mother refuses to say. Later when he's grown to manhood, he goes off to find him. Oh, the money of mortals! Oh, your riches — unless you're raking it in, you're never happy! I'm going in — not out of any devotion to the woman but for Clerus, who grew up on my milk and my hard work.

Dynamis Nutrix et Macrothyma vicina [58]

DI.   Mortalium casus,[59] quisquis ille patiatur, nostros arbitror. Hanc tamen mulierem non multifeci, sed filium, qui hinc abest, qui nos amat, caras habet. Sin istic adesset, multi suis se ditabunt qui minores forent. Maternum genus non hic pro cognato Clerum habet; pro peregrino potius. Sic ille vidit. Quandoquando veniat, res suas imminutas comperiet.

MA.   Nostra cum ferenda sint aequo animo, quid aliena iudicas?

DI.   Plura aecastor pro amicis debemus, quae nostram dignitatem minus attingerent. Non ego damnum nunc defleo mulieris, sed infortunium adulescentis,[60] qui si patrem minus convenerit, locum habebat ubi bene et laute viveret. At si differt, ista dilapidabunt.

MA.   Non ista curat. Magnanimus est nimis.

DI.   Magnanimus vix esse potest quis prae plurium moribus. Ubi se videt quis nihilifieri, pone saepius patiatur, victus tandem moribus vulgi ad ingenium redit.

MA.   Quot videmus mortalium divitias qui contemnunt, qui se bonis abdicant et durant, quoad spiritus illos depascit!

DI.   Fuerunt et hodie sunt. Tamen observantia religionis de vulgo coluntur, quamobrem se fructum pecuniarum possidere rentur. At si secundum philosophos, non religiosos, viverent, primum sentirent dedecus, famem, et opprobrium. Non paterentur, crede, Macrotima.

---

[58] Gloss: ἡ μακρόθυμη. patiens [macrothyma: long-suffering].

[59] *casus.* This word means an event or occurrence, often undesirable; and also includes the idea of fortune or misfortune. Again *Fortuna* is evoked.

[60] Plautus: *Captivi* 139–140: Egon non defleam / talem adulescentem?

[SCENE 5: BRITAIN]

Dynamis the Nurse and Neighbor Macrothyma

DY. No matter who's struggling with misfortune, it's our misfortune, too, I think. I didn't hold this woman in very high regard, but her absent son loves us and holds us dear. Without him present, his shirttail relatives will make themselves rich. His mother's family won't treat Clerus as one of their own; rather as a foreigner. And so he seems. If and when he gets back, he'll find his business affairs in dire straits.

MA. We have to bear our own fortunes as best we can. Why judge the affairs of others?

DY. By Castor, we owe friends many more things that touch less on our good names. I'm weeping not for the loss of the woman now, but for the misfortunes of the boy. If he hadn't sought his father, he'd have a place where he could live happily and well off. But if he doesn't get here soon, his inheritance will be gobbled up.

MA. He never paid attention to business. He's too generous.

DY. He can hardly be generous with that bunch, given the morals of most of them. When he finds himself with nothing, more often than not stabbed in the back, then conquered at last by their ways, he'll sink to the level of this mob.

MA. How many mortals we see who scorn riches, harden themselves and reject good things, until their bitter hearts consume them.

DY. That type is always around. Then there are the ones who think they'll get rich because they keep their religious observances. But if they lived by the philosophers instead of the priests, they'd end up ashamed, hungry, and disgraced. Believe me, Macrothyma, they couldn't bear it.

MA. Sed quid? Mulier ist‹a›ec nupta vidua vixit?[61]

DI. Vixit.

MA. Domi sola?

DI. Minime. Pedisequas habuit illa compluris.

MA. Quas? Aut cuiatis?

DI. Mechiam, Hyperiphaniam, Pleonexiam.[62]

MA. Tace, si me amas. Non miror quod saepius in hanc igitur invehant augures.
     Manibus istae frequenter ministrant. Hui, nollem haec mihi fuisset amica.

DI. Non tua fuit, neque mea. Unum hoc, unum ta‹n›tum boni peperit Clerum
     nostrum, cui spero boni plurimum, modo mea praecepta servet, ut
     consuerat.

MA. Periculum est huic, si paupertatem incidit. Nihil peius est homini, in divi-
     tiis qui nutritus sit. Ut argentum amittit, fraudes machinatur et dolos,
     furta, rapinas. Timendum est homini.

DI. Foret. Sed illum ego nutrivi.

MA. Tu quid me foras evocari iussisti?

DI. Ut casum scires de matre Cleri.

MA. Scivi.

DI. Tantum volui. Stultum fuit quippe nimis.

MA. Unde invalitudo tanta?

DI. Labiles sunt mulieres. Divitiae enervant homines. Discessit filius, et illius
     sibi pater in mentem venit. Tandem sic crevit aegritudo ut mortem obiret.
     Vellem id sciret noster Clerus.

MA. Quando istud fieri nequit, quod sors fert feramus.

DI. Sic factura fui.

MA. Consule cognatis mulieris, quod bona Clero fideliter tueantur.

DI. Non possum. Familiarita‹tem› meam penitus fugiunt. Dinamin si dixeris,
     infortunium dixeris.

MA. Me igitur quid facere vis?

DI. Ut mea scias, et familiariter amiceque vivamus.

MA. Sic fecero. Nonquid aliud me vis?

DI. Ut valeas.

MA. Et tu vale.

---

[61] Plautus: *Menaechmi* 726: Quin vidua vivam quam tuos mores perferam.

[62] M[o]echia means fornication; Hyperiphania, arrogance; Pleonexia, greed.

MA. But tell me. This married woman lived like a widow?

DY. She did.

MA. All alone in the house?

DY. Not at all. She had servants.

MA. Who are they, from what country?

DY. Mechia, Hyperiphania, Pleonexia.

MA. This isn't for everyone's ears. But it wouldn't surprise me if they routinely brought in someone to interpret the omens. Those servants often doctor her themselves. Oh, I could wish this woman weren't my friend.

DY. She wasn't really your friend or mine either. She bore only one son, such a good son — our Clerus, I hope all the best for him — but may he continue to follow my advice, as he'd been accustomed to doing.

MA. If he ends up with nothing, he's in trouble. Nothing's worse for someone who's been raised around money. When he loses it, he falls back on scams, tricks, thievery and stealing. You have to expect the worst for somebody like that.

DY. You're so right. But I nursed him, you know.

MA. Why did you have me come outside here?

DY. So you'd know the troubles of Clerus's mother.

MA. I knew already.

DY. As I wished. Oh, it's so ridiculous.

MA. Where does such foolishness come from?

DY. Women are frail. Wealth weakens people. Her son left, and she keeps thinking about his father. Finally, it weighs on her so heavily that she'd rather be dead. I wish our Clerus knew.

MA. When we can't make that happen, we have to bear with what chances.

DY. As I've always had to.

MA. Consult with the woman's family so her estate will be kept intact for Clerus.

DY. I can't. They completely shun me. If you say my name, you say misfortune.

MA. What do you want me to do, then?

DY. Know my situation. Live in friendship and trust with me.

MA. Consider it done. Isn't there anything else you need from me?

DY. That you should be well.

MA. And you.

R⟨H⟩ODI

Lorarius et Aristopistes servus [63]

LO. Mea quanquam sic fata velint quod per alienas calamitates vitam degam, non me credas adeo ferum, adeo inhumanum ut gaudeam malis et adversis tuis. Sed sum et sub alieno imperio vivo. Sic mandatum, sic facio. Immo, ut bene scias sententiam meam, nemo iam duos annos ad tonsorem venit cuius me magis miseritum sit atque tui.

AR. Ad tonsorem?

LO. Ita. Non sic in Belgis canes tondet ille tonsor: cui bellum indixerunt, ac lanam et corium hac in tonstrina infortunati plerique missum faciunt. V⟨a⟩e homini qui deducitur istuc! Si tamen e consilio meo feceris, moerores, quantum in te fuerit, depones, omniaque fortia et iniusta mala sperabis. Si quid paucioris venerit, id de lucro venerit.[64]

AR. Si me l⟨a⟩etum dixero, non arbitror credibile propter te videri. Moereo et doleo sic iniuste tractari. Sed hoc mihi magis dolet: quod, cum certa dicam, non credunt, quanquam lingua, mores, habitus, pellis satis testimonii afferant. Si dixero vero quod in ultimis pene terris mihi rerum sit nobilitatis et imperii, mihi quo pacto fidem dabunt?

LO. Cuiatis es?

AR. Apud Belgas natus. Unus est mihi pater de principibus maioribus.

---

[63] Gloss: Lorarius nomen est Latinum et est loris percussor id est flagel⟨l⟩o vel carceris custos ut hic et erat homo utriusque officii, et ὁ ἀριστόπιστης, -ου vir perfectae fidei. [The name Lorarius is Latin and means a striker, that is, with a whip, or a prison guard as here, and he was a man of each office, and aristopistes (most faithful), a man of perfect loyalty.]

[64] *De lucro venerit* resonates ironically with *de lucro vivere*, 'to be lucky to be alive.' See the *OLD* entry for *lucrum*. Thus the translation, "Then you'll come out a/head."

[Scene 6:] Rhodes

Lorarius and Aristopistes [*in chains*]

LO.   Although my fates dictate that I pass my life in strange calamities, don't think I'm so cruel and inhuman that I enjoy your difficulties and misfortunes. But here I am, living under a foreign rule. So what I'm told to do, I do. Really, now, so you'll know my mind, in two years I haven't sent anyone to the shearers that I've felt as sorry for as you.

AR.   Shearers?

LO.   Right. These shearers don't clip dogs like the Belgians do: when they declare war on their victim in this shop, he loses just about all of his wool and hide. Any man who gets taken to that place has had it! But if you take my advice, lay down the griefs that are heavy in you, and expect all things bold as well as undeserved disasters. But if what comes is too little, then you'll come out ahead.

AR.   When I described myself as well off, I don't think you really believed me. Being dragged around unjustly like this brings on grief and sorrow. But what's worse is, people don't believe me when I tell them the truth — even though the way I talk and dress and carry myself are all character witnesses. So if I said that in a distant country I'm deeply involved with the ruling class and the doings of government, how could they confirm that?

LO.   What country?

AR.   Born among the Belgians. My father's one of the upper nobility.

LO.   Ain vero?

AR.   Vero. Ne credant, quanquam longinqui simus, quod hic me sin habebunt male, quin et mei de vobis vindictas quaerant.

LO.   Tot sunt medii montes, tanta nos maria dividunt, ut huiuscemodi minus speranda sient.

AR.   Audi. Britan‹n›icum est mare nostrum, quod navigamus multis et immensis navibus.

LO.   Sua ist‹a›ec. Mea nihil interest. Mihi non succenseas, qui mandata exequor.

AR.   Tibi nihil ego quicquam succenseo, qui ingrate facias.

LO.   Immo invite.

AR.   Quid ergo gratum esset magis animo tuo: vel aetatem carnuficinae servire quod nunc agis, aut in divitiis et honoribus honeste vivere?

Quod bonum, scio tamen, quodque malum longissime.

LO.   Quisque bonum optat.[65]

AR.   Si quis te divitem faceret et fortunatum?

LO.   Hominem amarem.

AR.   Te ipsum ama.

LO.   Facio.

AR.   Feceris, ubi divitem tua te sapientia feceris.

LO.   Tantum nescio.

AR.   At ego te docebo, si meis dictis auscultabis.

LO.   Auscultabo.

AR.   Est mihi pater princeps in patria magnus.

LO.   Est. Quid ultra?

AR.   Magnus est terrarum orbis quem suo regit imperio.

LO.   Audio.

AR.   Si beneficium contuleris gnato suo, non fuerit tam ingratus quin tibi rem faciat simul et imperium. Porro meam effigiem plane specta, sin in me ingratitudinem fore speres. Quum ad me redibit imperium, participem te quoque fecero: quod etiam de parente non dubito impetrare posse ut faciat.

---

[65] Cf. Aristotle, *Nicomachean Ethics* I.1.1: Omnia appetunt bonum.

LO.   Are you telling me the truth?

AR.   Absolutely. Even though we're a long way away, if they thought I was being manhandled, they'd be here extracting a little revenge from the locals on my behalf.

LO.   There's lots of mountains between here and there, lots of seas. Not much hope of that.

AR.   Listen. The Britannic Sea is ours because we sail many ships across it, huge ships.

LO.   To each his own. It doesn't matter to me. Don't get mad at me, but orders are orders.

AR.   I'm not mad at you for anything, doing this is no fun for you.

LO.   Right, I just hate it.

AR.   Then what would you prefer — to spend your life in the torturer's trade, like now, or live honest, rich and respected?

[*Lorarius yawns*]

But I know good and evil seem a long way off.

LO.   Each man wants the good.

AR.   And if someone turns you lucky and makes you rich?

LO.   He'd be my friend for life.

AR.   Then shake hands with yourself.

LO.   I do.

AR.   You will, when you wise up and make yourself rich.

LO.   I don't know what you're getting at.

AR.   But I'll explain it, if you'll listen to what I'm saying.

LO.   I'm all ears.

AR.   My father is a great prince in our country.

LO.   Right. What else?

AR.   The lands under his personal rule are immense.

LO.   I'm listening.

AR.   If you do his son a good turn, he won't be ungrateful and hold back his wealth and power. Study this face of mine carefully, if you're afraid I'll be ungrateful. When I inherit that power, you'll get a piece of it, too: there's not a doubt in my mind my father will do it.

LO.   Ni me fallit indoles in te quae sita est, haud versutus es et callidus. Verum
      quum in laboribus sumus et alterius beneficio nobis opus est, boni. Ubi
      rem nacti sumus, ex bonis mali et fraudulentissimi ilico sumus facti.[66]

AR.   Ita me sancta libertas incolumem restituat ad patriam et ad patrem, uti tibi
      non minus fidelis fuero quam mihi, postquam beneficio tuo boias istas et
      compedes reliquero suis dominis.

LO.   In tantum iter argentum magnum non satis esse posset. Maximo foret
      opus. Tu quod habebas, perdidisti. Pauper ego sum. Unde argentum tan-
      tum comperiam miser?

AR.   Modo sit satis in Creten. Illic perire nequeo. Deposui plurimum apud
      C‹h›risolum argentarium.

LO.   Quid istas tu regiones visisti?

AR.   Dicam tibi. Rudis est, ignarus, et superbus, qui nisi suos viderit. Se suos-
      que viros credit, caeteros negligit et contemnit et saepius odit. Ego autem,
      istuc nonnunquam qui de parente perceperim, volvi periculum istuc de me
      fieri: quid alienae terrae sapiant. Abii de meis cum solo comite, qui fidelis
      fuit. Nonquid venit, de me ut persentis‹c›eret quid esset?

LO.   Non.

AR.   Sibi timuit ergo.

LO.   Sic arbitror, si cum peregrino verba fecit. Pessimus est rumor qui de nos-
      tris volat.

AR.   Unde igitur peregrini multi?

LO.   Spe lucri. Verum multi lanam ponunt.

AR.   Auri maledicta sitis![67] Hinc damna, naufragia, bella, latrones, insidiae, cae-
      teraque mundi mala.

LO.   Hinc vado ad portum ut visam an noctu navis ulla de Rhodo solvatur.
      Non istuc agamus luci.

AR.   Fiat.

---

[66] Plautus: *Captivi* 232–237: Nam fere maxima pars morem hunc homines habent: quod sibi volunt
/ dum id impetrant, boni sunt; / sed id ubi iam penes sese habent, / ex bonis pessimi et fraudu-
lentissimi / fiunt. . . . / Quod tibi suadeam, suadeam meo patri.

[67] Virgil: *Aeneid* 3.57: auri sacra fames.

LO. I may be wrong about you, but I don't think you're all that cunning and quick. But if we're in dire straits and we need help from someone, we can look like *such* good people. Then when we've gotten what we want, we change on the spot — from good to bad, or just plain deceitful.

AR. Listen, once I'm free and head for home and my father, I'll treat you like you were me. I'll leave these collars and shackles behind for your bosses because you helped me.

LO. Even a *lot* of money could fall short on a trip like that. It would be a very expensive proposition. What you had you've lost, and I'm not rich. Where's a poor, hard-working executioner like me going to find money like that?

AR. Ah, but there's enough in Crete. I can't lose there. I deposited more money than we'll need with Chrisolus the banker.

LO. When were you in those parts?

AR. Let me tell you something. A man who won't believe unless he sees with his own eyes is a fool — ignorant and overbearing. He believes only himself or his own people, others he ignores and despises, even hates. My father told me about this place, but I considered the danger, how people in foreign lands think. I brought only one companion, and he's been devoted. Couldn't he come along, so he could find out exactly what's going to happen to me?

LO. No.

AR. And so he feared for his own safety.

LO. Of course he did, if he talked with another traveler. The worst rumors about us are always flying around.

AR. Then why so many travelers?

LO. They hope they'll strike it rich. But most get sheared.

AR. That awful thirst for gold! It brings injuries, shipwrecks, wars, thieves, ambushes and all the other evils of the world.

LO. I'm going to the harbor to see if a ship sails from Rhodes tonight. We don't want to go to the pier in daylight.

AR. Right.

LO. Verum ne quis nostros dolos praesentiscat, te sic vinctum linquo. Non dormibis tamen amplius sic munitus. Ne dubita.

AR. Me tibi commendo.

LO. Pollicitus sum. Servare in eo stat quod dixi fidem.

AR. Memorem dices et gratum.

LO. I intro.

AR. Eo.

LO.   But so no one figures out our scheme beforehand, I'll just leave you chained like this. You'll never sleep better, nice and secure like this. Take my word for it.

AR.   You're too good to me.

LO.   I've promised. I've given my word — I'll stay the course.

AR.   You'll say I remember and I'm grateful.

LO.   Inside.

AR.   Going.

CRETES

Rhystes senex, Presbites et Elpis ancilla[68]

RHY. Sunt qu‹i› noxis gaudeant et exultent delictis suis. Ego, quia peccavi, noctes diesque maceror, tabesco peregrinus virginem fefelli.[69] Uxorem duxi plus quae minus nequeat nubere, gravidamque feci filio. Quem non ausus fuerim in hanc terram deportari prae huius formidine, quam secundam uxorem duxi. O ignaviam hominis! Non sat erat puellam fallere, quin et vicem dolis lactarem quoque, lege quae mea nequaquam esse potest. At dii, omnium protectores bonorum et custodes et malorum ultores, sterilem fecere Piichin de novo matrimonio. Gnatus nullus fuit. Et ulciscuntur iniurias quoque dii. Me qui liberos ex vero coniugio flocifecerim, alienos pro meis nutrire, coniugis natam Anapausim virginem mehercle forma et multis curis. Amatur de multis. Casta quidem est et pudica. Verum parum habeo fidei mulieribus, ubi Venus agitur, ubi amatores veniunt, ubi blanda loquuntur, ubi dexteras copulant, ubi oscula iungunt. O nimiam licentiam![70]

---

[68] Gloss: ὁ ῥύστης, -ου liberator est [rhystes: deliverer, one who sets free], et ὁ πρεσβὺς, -υος καὶ ὁ πρεσβίτης, -ου legatus vel senex [presbys: ambassador, and presbites: ambassador or an old man].

[69] Plautus: *Captivi* 133–134: Ego, qui tuo maerore maceror, / macesco, consenesco et tabesco miser.

[70] Terence: *Adelphoe* 508–509: verum nimia illaec licentia / profecto evadet in aliquod magnum malum.

[SCENE 7:] CRETE

Old Rhystes, Presbites [his slave], and

Elpis the Serving Maid

RHY. [*alone on stage*] There are those who rejoice in their wrongs and celebrate their sins. But I, because I've strayed, because I deceived a young girl when I was a traveler, night and day I'm tormented and I waste away. Then, when she couldn't have been less ready for a wedding, I made her my wife and got her pregnant with a son. I wouldn't dare bring him to this country to face the terror of that woman – yes, I've taken a *second* wife. Oh, I'm one sleazy character! I didn't just bed the girl, I deliberately led her on with a wedding, without a thought for our vows. But the gods, the guardians of the good and the whipmasters of the wicked, have made Epiichis barren, a disaster for the new marriage. We never had a child. And the gods have really revenged these wrongs. I, who cared not a whit about that child of a true marriage, now nourish someone else's child as my own — the young Anapausis, my wife's daughter — beautiful, by Hercules, and the cause of many cares. She's chased by many young men. But she's chaste indeed, and modest. Oh, I admit it, I have too little faith in women, when Venus is aroused, when lovers come to court, to whisper sweet nothings and hold hands, when their lips meet — Oh, wanton,

O praeparationes Veneris![71] Modo mea foret, non essent ingratae solli-
citudines. Dedecus esset meum, decus est aliorum.

Presbiten in Britan‹n›icum misi. Non venit. Iam annus abiit. Nec satis erat
dispendium viae, ni merces quoque dedissem. Sed sic faciundum fuit.
Praesentisset uxor.

EL.   Me miseram! Sic quamque misere herum video cruciarier. Nec causam
novi, nisi quod maturam viro videt Anapausim. Stulte faciunt aecastor qui
viduas ducunt, maxime si gregem habent. At fors ist‹a›ec magna fuit, nati
quod minus sunt novi liberi. Novi fuissent hero grati, Anapausis matri.
Tum frequenter illae turbae. "Cur non meam amas? Me miseram! Tum
mortua essem quum te primum duxi."[72] Gratias agant diis, quod haud
fecunda fuit.

RHY.   Si filium duceret, licebis filiam hanc pro mea educaverim, pati non posset
uxor quod in tecto viveret. Et ego dotem de meo suae dedero. O fortunatum qui caste vivit! Iam haec noxa de mente non abest. Ut primum c‹a›es-
pito, causam ascribo: quod Erichiam fraudavi.

PRE.   Non audeo Rhistem pene convenire, cuius ego legationem vanam fructu-
que cassam fecerim. Quid de mercibus dicam? Nec merces nec precium
adduco. Quid dicam huic? Satius est ante praemeditari quam inconsidera-
tum et in errore videri. Quid dicam? Dicam sic? Non credet. Quid si sic?
Non est vero simile. Quid si sic? Facilius credi potest.

---

[71] The first use of *Venus* in this speech seems to indicate the process of falling in love, with its other meaning, coition, hovering in the background. A series of terse clauses follows, obviously building to a culmination. Both *copulant* and *iungunt*, ending that series, mean generally *to join*, but now have become relevant in their more specialized sexual significance. Through Rhystes's obvious narrowing of thought, the second use of *Veneris*, set apart within its apostrophe, can only signify the sexual act. This piece of dialogue is an elegant bit of playwriting because it is so trenchantly dictated by character: in the course of his life Rhystes has gone from a sexually preoccupied *adulescens* to a sexually preoccupied *senex*. As his lines make quite clear, he is the quintessential dirty old man.

[72] Plautus: *Asinaria* 886: Non edepol conduci possum vita uxoris annua.

intemperate! Oh, prelude to more, much more! And from what I can tell, they're not unwelcome entreaties either. Honor's for others — for me there's shame.

[*Moves to the other side of the stage*]

I sent Presbites into Britain. It's been a year now, and he doesn't return. There wasn't enough for the cost of the trip, I didn't even furnish the goods. But it had to be done that way. My wife was getting suspicious.

EL.　[*Enters inner above, sees Rhystes*] Talk about miserable! Every day I watch the master go through hell. But why? Maybe it's when he sees the blossoming Anapausis with some young man. By Castor, it's fools who marry widows, especially if they've got a flock of children. But in a way it was lucky, because they didn't have children of their own. New children would have been welcome to the master and Anapausis's mother. But then the arguments came one on top of the other. "Why don't you love my daughter? This is pure misery, the day I married you I might as well have died." They should thank the gods she *didn't* have children.

RHY.　I get to raise this girl as my own, but if she marries a young man, the wife couldn't bear having him under our roof. And I'd have to set a dowry on her from my own money. Celibates are the lucky ones! And now I can't get it out of my head that this is my punishment. Whenever I stumble, I assign a reason: because I deceived Erichea.

[*As Rhystes exits into the house, Presbites enters main stage*]

PR.　I don't dare approach Rhystes. I failed the mission he gave me and I'm coming back empty-handed. What can I tell him about the goods? I don't have merchandise or anything else of value. What can I say? It's better to appear shrewd than thoughtless and wrongheaded. But what can I say? Whatever I tell him, he won't believe me. If I say one thing? It won't seem true. If I say something else? It could very easily be believed.

Satis est. Iam bene enumeravi rationes meas. Bonus est ille vir, quamvis adulescens peccaverit. Non dubito quin mihi credat, et tacitum et quietum suarum rerum reddat. At si secus faciat, causam ego deferam omnem ad uxorem. Mihi prospectem quidem opus est et necessarium. Accedam ad hostium. Pultabo fores.

EL. Quis hic ad nos recta tendit? Presbites aedepol est, qui nostras merces hinc devexit. Et novas ut opinor ipse detulit. Iam hoc est quod gaudeam. Nunc herus moerores parumper deponet.

PRE. Ecquis aperit hostium?

EL. Quis ad fores est? Presbites, te advenisse salvum gaudemus.

PRE. Credo. Et tu quoque salve. Ecquid omnes bene valetis?

EL. Recte.

PRE. Est Rhistes domi?

EL. Ellum istic ante hostium.

RHY. Quis a nobis exit? Ni me fallunt oculi, Presbites est. Is est! Presbites, advenisse salvum te volupe[73] est.

PRE. Salve, Rhistes.

RHY. Quid merces nostrae?

PRE. Non secundae nimis.

RHY. Abeamus hinc paululum ab aedibus.

PRE. Fiat.

RHY. Vidistin Erichiam?

PRE. Ad Stiga meandum erat.

---

[73] At its entry for the adverb *volup*, the *OLD* hypothesizes that the word's source is *volupe*, neuter of an old adjective, *volupis*, pleasurable. It then recommends a comparison with ἐλπίς, the Greek word from which Frulovisi has taken the personal name of the serving maid. Rhystes's use of *volupe* to describe Presbites's return speaks both to his knowledge of the two servants' intimate relationship and his own preoccupation with things sexual. Neither Plautus nor Terence employ *volupe*, but both use *volup*. But there is more to be mined here. Although this is the first scene in which Elpis appears, Frulovisi does not include the etymology of her name with those of the other characters at this scene's headnote. Perhaps he sought to avoid calling attention to the disjunction between *volupe* (pleasurable) and ἐλπίς (hope) that had developed over time. It is in the headnote of the following scene that Frulovisi glosses her name's Greek source for the first time. Moreover, since no one who was not deeply learned in Greek and Latin would apprehend these esoteric linkages from simply listening at a performance, it seems reasonable to infer that Frulovisi expected his comedies to be studied in detail by scholars.

[*brightening*]

Okay. I've got my story straight. He's a good man, even though he strayed in his youth. He'll believe me, sure — and things will settle down. But if it falls apart, I'll blame everything on his wife. Whatever happens, I've got to look out for myself. Give way to the enemy's strength, that's it. I'll knock on the door.

EL.   Who's coming here straight toward us? By Pollux, it's Presbites! Oh, he's brought our merchandise here, he's brought the new goods down himself. Now it's my turn to grin. Now the master will put away that long face for a bit.

[*Elpis exits inner above. Presbites knocks*]

PR.   Won't anyone open the door?

EL.   [*Enters from the house*] Who's at the door? Presbites! Thank the gods you've arrived safely!

PR.   I think I have. Greetings to you, too. All's well with you?

EL.   Oh, yes.

PR.   Is Rhystes home?

EL.   [*Rhystes enters from the house*] Here he comes now.

RHY.   Who's this? If my eyes don't deceive me, it's Presbites. Yes, it's him! Presbites, how delightful that you've arrived safely.

PR.   Greetings, Rhystes.

RHY.   What news of our merchandise?

PR.   Nothing overly favorable.

RHY.   Let's go over here, away from the house.

PR.   As you will.

[*Elpis exits*]

RHY.   Did you see Erichea?

PR.   She has passed on to the River Styx.

RHY. Mortua est?

PRE. Est.

RHY. Quid illius partus?

PRE. Puer natus est. Modo vir est.

RHY. Vidistin?

PRE. Minime. Nam cum audivisset eius patrem vivere, te quaesitum ivit. Hinc
matris omnis morbus, omnis invalitudo, pestis denique.

RHY. Solus?

PRE. Cum uno comite, Aristopiste servo.

RHY. Pergunt huc recta?

PRE. Matrem nusquam potuit exorare, qua tu patria natus fores. Invita parente
se fortunam quaerere dixit. Abierunt dites, ut audio.

RHY. Me miserum, turbas qui tanti facerem uxoris, proprie quae non erat uxor,
ut gnatum flocifacerem! O gnate mi, quas terras peragrabis, quot hostes
habebis, quibus vita tibi fuerit subiecta periculis!⁷⁴

PRE. A‹r›istopistes ille servus maior est natu puero, mirum in modum astutus,
callidus, et fidelis tamen⁷⁵ quas ob res minus adulescenti timendum puto.

RHY. Deos oro quod illi bene fuat. Sed me semper m‹o›morderit animus quod
filium genui, mea qui causa tot in pericula vadat, labores, calores, frigora,
latrones, ignaros peregrinis semper hostis. Non arbitror in futurum mihi
plus boni fore.⁷⁶

PRE. Ne dubita, et illum forte videbis et brevi. Magna est similitudo morum liberum atque parentum. Id mihi credas velim. Fortunam quaerit. Nulla sibi
grata fuerit, ni propter te vivat. Maxima est quam in te, qua‹m›vis incog-
nitum, pietas gerit.

RHY. Sic fore velim. Verum quid nostrae merces valent? Quid emolumenti
devexisti?

---

⁷⁴ At *Aeneid* 6.692–693, Anchises speaks to his son Aeneas: Quas ego te terras et quanta per aequora
vectum / accipio! quantis iactatum, nate, periclis!

⁷⁵ Plautus: *Amphitryon* 268: Itaque me malum esse oportet, callidum, astutum admodum. *Pseudolus*
385–386: Ad eam rem usust homine astuto, docto, cauto et callido, / qui imperata ecfecta reddat, non
qui vigilans dormiat.

⁷⁶ Plautus: *Rudens* 504: Ubi perdidi etiam plus boni quam mihi fuit.

RHY. Dead then?

PR. She is.

RHY. And the child?

PR. A son, now very nearly a man.

RHY. Did you see him?

PR. Impossible. When he heard his father was alive, he went to seek you. Then the mother was ravaged by disease and sickness, and at the end, the plague.

RHY. Was the boy alone?

PR. One traveling companion, a slave, Aristopistes.

RHY. Will he proceed directly here?

PR. He could never get his mother to tell him what country you were from. Since his mother was unwilling, he said he'd seek his fortune himself. They left with quite a bit of money, as I hear.

RHY. What a mess I've made. I carried on so much about my wife, though I didn't treat her like a wife at all, that I completely forgot the boy! Oh, son — you'll wander alien lands, face enemy after enemy, your very life will be in danger!

PR. That slave Aristopistes is older than the boy. They say he's smart, level-headed and loyal, so I'm not too worried about the boy.

RHY. I pray the gods let it go well for him. But my heart will always gnaw at me because I know my son, on account of me, rushes into dangers, trials, heat, cold, robbers — always the unknown enemies of travelers. Nothing good will ever happen to me again.

PR. Put aside your doubts, and you just might see him soon. There's a strong resemblance between these foolish children and their parents, believe me. He seeks his fortune. He'll never be happy with himself unless he settles down near you. His respect for you is immense, even though he hasn't even met you.

RHY. I hope you're right. But what are our goods worth? How much did they bring?

PRE.   Non multum. Neminem ego fidum comeri. Vix in com‹m›eatum fuere in nostram patriam. Praeterea et Ausoniam circumivi, mitto Gallias, Germanias, Il‹l›iricum, Thes‹s›aliam. Volui tuum ad te deducere filium. Cum autem argentum iam defuturum timerem, redii.

RHY.   Nec aliter credidi. O infortunatum me! O infelicem! Damnum istud primum est maximum: quod deliqui. Gnatum perdidi, argentum, rem. Precium ob dolos tuli. Tu mihi sic rem ministrasti. Actum est profecto. Certum est non rem amplius curare, non amicos, non cognatos. Hinc ab oculis abi tuis cum legationibus!

PRE.   Eo. Quid ille faciet mihi? Si mihi molestus esse perget, faciam ego quod, dum ipse vivat, os habeat quod in dies rodat semper suos. Non credo tam demens siet ut mihi dicam scribat. Bona sunt iura possidentis. Sed cesso ad uxorem meam pergere, quae me plus amat quam oculos suos.[77]

---

[77] See note 42.

PR.   Not much. I don't have anyone under contract for them. They hardly ever do business in our country. Besides that I scoured Italy, to say nothing of France, Germany, Illyria, Thessaly. I wanted to bring your son to you. But when I got worried that the money would run out, I came back.

RHY. I believe you, of course. Oh, I'm unlucky! Unhappy! This loss is first and foremost because of that old transgression. My son, my money, and my business are all gone. That's the price of my deceptions. You took care of the business end for me. And oh, what a mess. Certainly no one could have handled the affair quite like you did, not friends, not family. Get your baggage and business sense out of my sight!

PR.   I go. [*Rhystes exits*] What's he going to do to me? If he starts trouble, I'll make sure his son and his money are on his mind every day of his life. I don't think he's so far gone he'll punish me with the law. An owner has absolute rights. But I draw the line at my wife, who loves me more than her own eyes.

Anapausis virgo et Elpis ancilla [78]

AN. Nescio quid mihi obiectum sit novi morbi. Mihimet, Elpis, mea Elpis, displic⟨e⟩o. Nec gusto cibum, nec somnum oculis video meis. Aegritudo, labor, moeror, mala omnia meo sedent in animo. Meae profecto vitae timeo. [79]

EL. Hem, quid istuc est quod audio? Vereor ne procedant ista ex nimio ocio.

AN. Nescio quid ocii narres. Ita me iuvet alma Iuno, quam deorum reginam metuo, quamque revereri et metuere est aequum, uti totas noctes defetiscor opere. Nec tamen somnus unquam venit. Me mori sentio. Ni quis medelam huic afferat aegritudini meae, peribo profecto.

EL. Quis te morbus agitat, hera?

AN. Nescio.

EL. Quid tibi dolere sentis?

AN. Aecastor praecordia tota.

EL. Sine quod attingam.

AN. Nihil quicquam invenies.

EL. Dixtin matri, illa quod medicum adduci iuberet.[80]

AN. Non.

---

[78] Gloss: ἡ ἀνάπαυσις, -εως est requies [anapausis is repose], et ἡ Ἐλπίς, -δος est spes [and elpis is hope, trust]. I thank Leslie S. B. MacCoull for pointing out that anapausis, "repose," was a favorite personification in Renaissance house decoration.

[79] Plautus: *Cistellaria* 59–61: Misera excrucior, mea Gymnasium: male mihi est, male maceror; / doleo ab animo, doleo ab oculis, doleo ab aegritudine. / Quid dicam, nisi stultitia mea me in maerorem rapi?

[80] Terence: *Hecyra* 323: Pam. Quid morbi est? Par. Nescio. Pam. Quid? Nemon medicum adduxit?

[SCENE 8: CRETE]

Young Anapausis and her Servant Elpis

AN. Elpis, I'm sick and I don't know what it is. Oh, Elpis, I'm turning myself melancholy. I can't eat, can't sleep. I'm sad, upset, depressed — all things bad hold my heart. I know I'll just die.

EL. Well, you don't say? If you ask me, this comes from too much idleness.

AN. I don't know what you mean by idleness. Gracious Juno helps me, I fear her as queen of the gods, it's right to reverence and fear her, I wear myself out using all my nights in prayer. But still sleep never comes. I feel as if I'm dead. If someone doesn't cure this illness of mine, I'll die.

EL. What illness has gotten hold of you, mistress?

AN. I don't know.

EL. What feels achy to you?

AN. By Castor, my entire breast.

EL. Let's see if I can figure it out.

AN. You won't find anything at all.

EL. You've told your mother she should send for the doctor?

AN. No.

EL.   Quin dicis!

AN.   Non ausim.

EL.   Qui?

AN.   Diceret: "Quid tibi dolet?"[81] At membra valent. "Est tibi febris?" Sin aio, exterior nulla videtur. Nemo melius, Elpis, mihi potest mederi quam fidus amicus. Medici non istos morbos curant.

EL.   Quis est?

AN.   Hei mihi! Non audeo dicere.

EL.   Quin dic quid est! Non satis mihi dum habes fidei? Ego pol per me sic studuisse credo, ut omnia tua iure mihi crederes. Sin aliter agis, infortunium, non est ea culpa mea.

AN.   Tibi credo. Verum pudet, nec lingua satis potest expedire.

EL.   Multa quidem eveniunt hominibus, hera, quae pudent eos, quaeque si tacerent, eorum in discrimen vita veniret. Quod patere mali, ne clam habeas iis qui tibi bene volunt. Si palam fiet, medelam conveniemus. Si clam, morbus fortassis aggravescet.

AN.   Nostin virginitatem meam, qualis siet?

EL.   Credo.

AN.   Quid bene credis?

EL.   Sedatum quod habeas cupidinem.

AN.   Oh!

EL.   Amat aedepol, aut vicii est illatum quicquam mulieri. Quid est. An vis est illata tibi abs quopiam improbo?

AN.   Ah, Elpis mea, minime.

EL.   Unde igitur haec suspiria trahis?

AN.   Dicam tibi.

EL.   Adsum.

AN.   Vidi.

EL.   Quid?

AN.   Peregrinum.

EL.   Perge.

AN.   Adolescentulum.

---

[81] Plautus: *Mercator* 368–369: Sed istuc quid est, tibi quod commutatust color? / Numquid tibi dolet?

EL.   And why not!

AN.   I wouldn't dare.

EL.   But why?

AN.   She'd say, "What ails you?" But my limbs are strong. "Do you have a fever?" Whatever I say, she won't be able to find symptoms. Elpis, no one can heal me better than my own dear love. Doctors don't cure *these* infirmities.

EL.   All right, who is he?

AN.   Oh, I'm so miserable! I don't dare say.

EL.   Tell me what's going on! Don't you trust me enough? By Pollux, I thought I've been on your side so much that you'd trust me with all your secrets. But if you'd rather not — well, don't blame the results on me.

AN.   Oh, I do trust you. Still, it's shameful, and words can't explain it very well.

EL.   Lots of things happen to people that make them blush, and if they bottle it all up their life comes to a turning point. Whatever it is that hurts, you shouldn't keep it from those who want the best for you. If it's brought out in the open, we can find a cure. But if it's kept deep inside, the illness could get worse.

AN.   Elpis — my maidenhood, what is it?

EL.   I think ...

AN.   What do you really think?

EL.   That you have a great longing.

AN.   [*deep sigh:*] Oh!

EL.   She's in love, by Pollux, or something's *really* wrong with the girl. That's it. Or are you just being stubborn?

AN.   Ah, my Elpis — don't.

EL.   So where are you pulling these sighs from?

AN.   I'll tell you.

EL.   Here I am.

AN.   I've seen —

EL.   What?

AN.   A traveler.

EL.   Go on.

AN.   A young man.

EL. Amat. Quid tum postea?

AN. Deum visa sum videre.

EL. Quando?

AN. Pridie.

EL. Ubi?

AN. Hic ante hostium.

EL. Solum?

AN. Immo cum patre una.

EL. Vidisti. Quid tum postea?

AN. Is me anima suppilavit.

EL. Quid ille? Ubi divertitur?

AN. Nescio. Istud triduum[82] frequens ante hostium steti, ut viderem virum, is nusquam. Hei mihi, vereor ne istinc abierit.

EL. Quid facturan? Morituran es, ni illum vides?

AN. Ne dubita.

EL. Hera, ubi tuus solitus animus, quae viros quosque soles spernere? Quotiens negabas mihi te virum amaturam unquam? Parce sodes. Unde haec nova dementia? Nunc amas, et nescis quem.

AN. Facile evenit quod diis est cordi. Saucia sum ego nimis. At viderem semel hominem saltem quaque die, nihil aliud cuperem. O pulchrum adulescentulum! O nobilem virum! Haud est iste nostrorum similis. Hominem quum videas, Apollinem credas. Dignitatem vereor viri, ne quis eripiat mihi.

EL. Nonquid memoria tenes illius effigiem? Quam si meministi, fac ut sciam. Plateas ego saepe visito. Dabo fortassis operam, quod scibis quid ex homine siet.

AN. Pulcre novi. Grandis est, rectus, propagatus, capillus crispus, facies divina, longa, non rufus, albus potius et flavus totus, latus pectore, in medio gracilis, rectissime et bene foratae tibiae.

---

[82] Frulovisi would likely attribute the apparent contradiction between Anapausis's use of *triduum* here and *pridie* just above it to the fact that she is awash in the confusions of young love.

EL.   She's in love, all right. So what happened?

AN.   It was like seeing a god.

EL.   When?

AN.   Yesterday.

EL.   Where?

AN.   Right here in front of the door.

EL.   Was he alone?

AN.   Not at all. He was with an old gentleman.

EL.   So you saw him. Then what happened?

AN.   He stole my heart.

EL.   Who is he? Where's he from?

AN.   I don't know. I've stood in front of the house constantly for three days now, to catch sight of the man, but he's nowhere to be seen. Oh me, I'm afraid he's moved on from here.

EL.   But what's to do? You'll die if you don't see him?

AN.   Oh, yes!

EL.   Mistress, hey — where's the old spirit? You used to give these guys the brushoff. How often have you sworn to me you'd never fall for any boy? Easy, please. Where's this new craziness from? Suddenly you're in love and you don't even know who he is.

AN.   Whatever the gods want, it happens just like that. Oh, I suffer so much. But if I could see the man just once each day I wouldn't want anything else. He's so handsome! Such a noble young man! He hardly resembles us mortals. When you see the man, you'll think he's Apollo. What if he's highborn and won't even look at me?

EL.   Don't you remember what he looks like? If you remember, tell me so I'll know. I'll keep checking the streets. And maybe I'll give myself the job of finding out what might come of this man.

AN.   I remember him well. Tall and straight, a well-proportioned body. Curly hair, a wonderful narrow face — not ruddy, more all white and gold — broad chest, slender waist, very straight and well-formed legs.

Vestis enim perbrevis est non philosophice vestit.

EL.   Quamdiu cum patre fuit?

AN.   Nescio. Parum ante hostium. Abiere post una uterque.

EL.   Facile collegisti effigiem hominis.

AN.   Quis non effecisset? Nescio quid elegantius viderim diebus meis.

EL.   Bono animo fac fuas. Ego diligenter hominem perquisivero, curaboque ut illum videas. Si res digna sit, cui tu nervos intendas tuos,[83] persuadebo matri sic, quod et ipsa patri, ut illi nubas.

AN.   Elpis, si feceris, nomen commutassis. Non ancillam, sed heram te modo dixero.

EL.   Tantum ex te nolo. Sat est quod mihi ex animo bene velis.

---

[83] Terence: *Eunuchus* 312: Sic adeo digna rest, ubi tu nervos intendas tuos.

[*Elpis gives her a look*]

Well, his tunic is very short.

[*Gives her another look*]

I mean, he doesn't wear a long gown like a philosopher.

EL.   How long has he been with the old gentleman?

AN.   I don't know. They hardly paused in front of the house. They left one right after the other.

EL.   You pulled together a description of the young man easily enough.

AN.   Who wouldn't? I don't think I've seen anything more wonderful in all my days.

EL.   Get your heart cheerful now. I'll search every nook and cranny for the man, and I'll make sure you see him. If it's a suitable match you're so het up about, I'll persuade your mother that, just as she married your father, so you should wed him.

AN.   Elpis, if you bring it off, you'll change your name. I'll call you mistress, not servant.

EL.   None of that from you now. Just wish me well from your heart and that's enough.

Epiichis mulier, Elpis ancilla, et Rhistes senex [84]

PI. Quid sperem? Sperem? Credin in animum inducere queam hunc, dicam virum an labores meros, quod me magnifaciat? Domi stat totos dies, et mu-
tum dicas, sin hominem vere spectes. Quid illi credis moerorum? Quid
aliud sollicitat virum, nisi quod mortem meam expetit[85] et natae meae? O
avariciam hominis!

Ego pol alias vidi mulieres quae aliter utuntur viris suis, et sunt interdum
quattuor natorum matres. Me miseram! Quid istuc est infortunii mei? Reor
istunc dotem meam spectare. Aedepol, quanquam vidua forem, iuvenis
eram tamen, quum illi data sum. Dos non multa fuit, at inerat forma. Tum
aliam dotem dedi, vero quae dos dici debet, pudicicia scilicet, sedatus cu-
pido, parentum, coniugis, et affinium amor.[86] Miseram me, quid in hunc
merita sum?

EL. Hera, quid te maceras? Quid tu has tuas omnes rationes in peiorem partem
trahis?[87] Nescin viros, quibus inest onus familiae, maximis implicari curis,
nec semper voluptatibus studere posse?

---

[84] Gloss: ἡ ἐλπίς, -δος spes [elpis: hope], ὁ ῥύστης, -ου liberator [rhystes: deliverer, one who sets
free]

[85] Terence: *Adelphoe* 874: Meam autem mortem expectant scilicet.

[86] Plautus: *Aulularia* 239: dum modo morata recte veniat, dotata est satis.

[87] Terence: *Eunuchus* 630–632: Ubi, quid in animost molestiae, / aliam rem ex alia cogitare et ea
omnia / peiorem in partem.

[SCENE 9: CRETE]

The Woman Epiichis, Elpis the maid, and Old Rhystes

EPI.   What's left for me to hope for? What? You'd think I could reach deep
down and find a little hope. Or say something nice about the man — his
sheer hard work, how he shares his money and his social standing with me.
But if you really watch the man, he stays home every day. Why is he so
happy being sad? What else stirs this man except waiting for me to die
and worrying about my daughter? Oh, the avarice of this man!

[Throws up her hands]

By Pollux, I've seen women put their men to work in a very different way,
and become mothers four times over. No such luck for me! What disaster's waiting for me round the bend? I think all he wanted was my dowry.
By Pollux, I may have been a widow when he got me, but I was still a
young woman. Oh, the dowry wasn't much, but a beautiful woman came
with it. And then I gave another dowry too, or something that should be
called a dowry: modesty of course, emotions in balance, and love of parents, spouse and kin. But look at me, what did it get me?

EL.   Mistress, why do this to yourself? Why drive your thoughts into a worse
state? You know men bear the burden for the family, they're all wrapped
up in heavy cares. They can't always be devoted to pleasures.

PI.   Quibus curis? An illi desunt sumptus quibus nos alat? Non est dives
satis?[88]

EL.   Ego bona venia tua dixero. Tu, modo quod optas impetrares, rem non ultra consideras. Iam ex te abiit illius iactura de mercatore suo Britan‹n›ico?

PI.   Primum autem, unde rusticitas tanta? Ingreditur. Neminem appellat. Ad
Acheronta statim illum credas profecturum. Nihil ego quicquam convenio
coniecturae, nisi quod aliam amat et meam mortem expetit, aut illum mor-
dent sumptus filiae.

RHI. Quid ego faciam miser? In miserias et erumnas me natum arbitror. Hoc
unum deerat: ut domi foret quae meam senectutem excruciaret.[89]

EL.   Nequeo satis istud in animum inducere quod verum siet. At pone sic esse.
Anapausis tua est iam matura viro. Locabitur. Ubi factum fuerit, desinet.

RHI. Quid faciam? Novi hominis ingenium huius. Sin illam placo, adversabor
quippe. Sin adversor sibi, persuadebit quod autumat. Adversabor potius.
Hoc est ingenium mulierum: asperis et contrariis, non adulationibus vin-
cu‹n›tur.[90] Sin illis te su‹m›mittis, actum est. Sin imperium tuum esse velis, minus contumaces evadent. Quid istuc est, quod iamdiu me accusas,
mulier?[91] An quod ea non utor libidine qua quum adulescentior fui? Credin homines semper eosdem esse? Sin illum me semper volebas, cur non
parcebas mihi magis? Nihil est tam durum tamque validum quod usu semper duret.

---

[88] Plautus: *Aulularia* 166: Ego virtute deum et maiorum nostrum dives sum satis. *Miles Gloriosus* 1063:
Non mihi avaritia umquam innatest: satis habeo divitiarum.

[89] Terence: *Andria* 886–887: Quor me excrucio? Quor me macero? / Quor meam senectutem huius
sollicito amentia?

[90] Terence: *Eunuchus* 812–813: Novi ingenium mulierum: / nolunt ubi velis, ubi nolis cupiunt ultro.

[91] The comic tension here lies in the formality of these exchanges, abetted by a kind of symmetrical
rhetorical design. As Rhystes begins the argument, he sets up the first of three repetitions of parallel
structure: the initial sentence of this and of the next two speeches begins with *quid*; in addition, the second sentence of each speech starts with *an* in its formal function of introducing the second of a series
of questions. Epiichis in the second speech goes him one better: where he had addressed her as *mulier*,
she invokes their formal relationship by addressing him as *mi vir*. In the third speech, Rhystes adopts her
more formal address with *mea uxor*. When Elpis interrupts their interchange, Rhystes shatters the high
formality and tense politeness of the moment by exploding at their slave.
See also Terence: *Heauton*. 622–624: Sos. Ehem mi vir. Chr. Ehem mea uxor. Sos. Te ipsum quaero.
Chr. Loquere quid velis. / Sos. Primum hoc te oro, ne quid credas me advorsum edictum tuom / facere
esse ausam.

EPI. What cares? Can't he support us? Isn't he rich enough?

EL. Let me give you some advice. As long as you get what you want, forget everything else. Up here — [*She taps her forehead*] — he's a million miles away, isn't he, because of his losses in Britain?

[*Rhystes enters*]

EPI. Just a second — why such rudeness? He comes in, and not a hello for anyone. You'd think he was at death's door. I don't put any stock in gossip, but he's either in love with someone else and hopes I'll die, or the expenses of a daughter are getting him down.

RHY. Why do I do this to myself? I think I was born into miseries and pain. Only one thing is missing — that what torments my old age should be in my own house.

EL. I can hardly believe it's true, but put it like this. Your Anapausis is now ripe for a husband. It's time to find her a match. The only thing up in the air is when it will happen.

RHY. [*aside:*] What should I do? She's as cunning as a man, I know that. To keep her calm, I'll really have to put up a fight. But even if I stand up to her, she'll fight for what she thinks. Well, I'll fight harder. Here's how it stands with women: they're conquered by harsh words and confrontations, not by sweet-talking them. If you give in, it's all over. But if you want to be your own boss, don't let these high-and-mighties get by with anything. [*to Epiichis*] Woman, what are you accusing me of now? Or maybe you think I don't have that passion I did when I was younger? But don't you know men will always be men? And if you were always wanting me yourself, why weren't you nicer to me? Nothing's as sturdy and strong as what's seasoned by constant use.

PI. Quid tibi venit in mentem, mi vir, ist‹a›ec in me dicere? An ego quando
     operam dedi quod minus viveres? Tibi semper morigera fui: quod par est
     mulieri.

RHI. Quid tibi venit in mentem, mea uxor, quod me insimulas avariciae? An tibi
     quicquam defuit meae domi, quod ad sumptus esset tibi tuaeque filiae?
     Nec tibi multum adversator fui.

EL. Here, non te accusat hera, verum dolet tuis moeroribus.

RHI. Ne te nostris admisceas rebus. Tu tua cura.[92]

PI. Solent alii coniugibus sua communicare.

RHI. Stulte faciunt.

PI. Cupio more.

RHI. Tuum est istuc.

PI. Certum est istuc. Meam mortem expetis. Quid tibi feci misera? Ita me su-
     peri iuvent, inferi, et medioxissimi,[93] uti nihil quicquam merita sum quod
     tu tantum in me caperes odii.[94] Tibi sum semper obsecuta. Gratum quod
     credidi, id feci; quod ingratum, minime.

RHI. Nescio quid dicas. Non odium ego cepi tui, mulier. Sin autem istiusmodi
     fueris, ex animo meo paulatim decides. Respice. Considera bene aetatem
     meam. Ipsa senectus aegritudines et moerores affert. Me divitem dicis. Nec
     satis est. Nullus est nobis verus heres, filius noster, qui meos in morte
     claudat oculos. Nec etiam quis est sic pecuniosus ut bonorum iacturam fa-
     cile patiatur. Presbites, bonus ille vir, quantum mihi rei dilapidavit!

PI. Ante illius adventum et is tu quidem eras.

RHI. Quantum distulit, nec litteras dedit! Vin in amore mecum vivere? Fac tu
     tibi persuadeas quod te diligam. Sin aliter potero suspicari, nec amabo te
     neque tuos.

PI. Istuc ego velim certum esset.

RHI. Erit, si mihi auscultabis. Hinc eo.

---

[92] The MS. reads: Ne te nostris admisceas rebus admisceas rebus. I have deleted the copyist's inad-
vertent repetition. Plautus: *Miles Gloriosus* 951: Quin tu tuam rem cura potius quam Seleuci. Terence:
Adelphoe 802: Quando ego tuom non curo, ne cura meum.

[93] Plautus: *Cistellaria* 512: At ita me di deaeque, superi atque inferi et medioxumi.

[94] Terence: *Hecyra* 580: Numquam sciens commerui, merito ut caperet odium illam mei.

EPI.　Dear husband, what comes into your head to say such things against me? Or maybe it's because I got out and did things while you were living life less? But I've always done what you wanted, that's a woman's lot.

RHY.　Dear wife, what comes into *your* head that you accuse me of being tight-fisted? Or if you lacked anything in my home, wasn't the money there for you and your daughter? And I've hardly ever said no to you.

EL.　Master, the mistress isn't accusing you, but she worries about your dark moods.

RHY.　You keep your nose out of our affairs. Mind your own business.

EPI.　It's customary with other husbands to talk things over with their wives.

RHY.　They're fools.

EPI.　I'd like what's customary, too.

RHY.　That's your problem.

EPI.　That's for sure. You're just waiting for me to die. But what did I ever do to you to deserve this? Now may those above, below, and right in the middle help me, no way have I deserved that you should hold me in such hate. I've always done what you asked. Whatever I thought would make you happy, I did it. Whatever I thought would be unwelcome, I didn't even consider.

RHY.　I don't know what you're talking about. I don't hate you, woman. But if you're going to carry on that way, little by little my love will fade away. But think now, consider well my years. This old age brings griefs and sorrows. Yet you call me rich. And that's not all. We have no true heir, a son of ours to close my eyes in death. What's more, nobody's so rich that he'll let his estate just go to the dogs. But Presbites, that good man, has just wrecked the most part of my business affairs!

EPI.　You were like this before he ever came back.

RHY.　He squandered everything, he didn't write! Do you want my affection? See you convince yourself I hold you dear! If I suspect otherwise, there'll be no love for you *or* yours.

EPI.　I wish your affection was certain.

RHY.　It will be, if you'll listen to me. I'm going out. [*Exits*]

PI.   Quid consulis, Elpis mea? Quid faciundum censes?[95]

EL.   Ego ex hominis moribus viverem, quantum in me foret. In obsequio forem.
        Tibi nunc ope sua quidem opus est, et magis opus quoad Anapausis bene
        locata siet.

PI.   Sic ergo faciam. Dii nos respiciant omnes. Ego ad filiam pergo. Tu quod
        parato opus est, para.

EL.   Fecero.

---

[95] This is a standard question inviting the articulation of the next attempt at controlling the plot,
usually, as here, answered by the clever slave. But, quite unusual in this instance, both characters are
women. See Plautus: *Amphitryon* 1128–1129: Ego Teresiam coniectorem advocabo et consulam / quid
faciundum censeat. *Menaechmi* 700: Ibo et consulam hanc rem amicos, quid faciendum censeant. *Mostellaria*
556: Th. Quid nunc faciundum censes? Tr. Egon quid censeam? Terence: *Eunuchus* 720: Sed nunc quid
faciundum censes, Doras?

EPI. What's your advice, Elpis? What do you think I should do?

EL. I'd live with the man's moods, as much as I had it in me. I'd be submissive. Right now you really need his help, especially while Anapausis is getting herself well situated.

EPI. Here's what I'll do then, all the gods watch over us. I'm going to concentrate on the daughter. You need to be prepared, get ready.

EL. Standing by.

Clerus adulescens et Rhistes senex[96]

CL. Hoc illud est quod ex omnibus sententiis meis falsum comperio. Qui in officio vivat, utique bene vivat. Ni fefellissem mulierem, modo iam periissem fame, vel nudus essem. Verum minuitur argentum.[97] Unde nobis vita fuerit? Istud durum. Quid apud Cretens‹e›s ego fecero? Quo proficiscar? Laudarier ego video bonos, et nimis infrigidarier. Audin, Clere? Nemo te novit istic. Si non potero quod volo, volam quod potero. Nequeo meo modo vivere? Vivam alieno.[98] Nulla est amplius quidem spernenda opera. Quo peius habebunt virtutem meam et precio minori, et ego minus apud illos fuero. Certum est officium nullum aspernare, modo vitam comperiam. Ego Cretenses alios viros credidi. Quum advenissem, rogari rebar, sed omnibus supplicato aedepol opus est. Fiat quod fortuna velit.

Quis istic est senex qui huc recta iter habet? Is est qui meum tam diligenter genus exquirit. Mihi credo uxorem dare velit. Peregrinus sum. Par est, istis quod me submissius habeam. Here, salve.

---

[96] Gloss: ὁ ῥύστης, -ου liberator [rhystes: deliverer, one who sets free].

[97] Literally, "Truly my money is diminished." An interesting alternate reading: "my true coin slips away."

[98] Terence: *Andria* 305–306: quoniam non potest id fieri quod vis, / id velis quod possit; 805: ut quimus, aiunt, quando ut volumus non licet; *Adelphoe* 739–741: ita vitast hominum quasi quom ludas tesseris: / si illud quod maxume opus est iactu non cadit, / illud quod cecidit forte, id arte ut corrigas.

[SCENE 10: CRETE]

Clerus the Young Man and Old Rhystes

CL.   [*alone*] Out of all my convictions, I find this is the one that doesn't ring true: he who lives a life of duty without doubt lives honorably. If I hadn't cheated that woman, I'd have already died of hunger, I'd be naked. And on top of that, my money's gone. What does life have in store for us? That's a hard one. What could I do here among these Cretans? But then where should I head for? I keep the company of good men to gain some praise, but they leave me out in the cold. Listen, Clerus, nobody knows you here. If I can't do what I want, I'll want what I can do. I can't live the way I'd like? Then I'll live a different way. [*with conviction:*] Nothing's more common than work left undone. That's why they'll hold my good name less and my reputation even lower, and I'll be pretty small change to them. But I can't just turn my back on my obligations if I'm going to find my way in life. I confided in some men of Crete when I arrived here. I thought I'd have my opinion sought out, but by Pollux I have to bow and scrape to everybody. Well, let Fortune work it out.

[*Rhystes enters*]

Who's that old man heading over here? He's the one who keeps asking about my family. I'd swear he wants to give me a wife. I'm a foreigner, so it's smart to be receptive to these offers. Greetings, good sir.

RHI. Fili, quid? Habes dum diverticulum?

CL. Apud hospitem meum argento meo.

RHI. Nec comeristi cui famulares?

CL. Non quem satis dignum ducerem officio meo.

RHI. Tu mihi, quod rogabam, noluisti dicere. Iam mecum esses sumptibus meis.

CL. Quid voluisti scire, quod non dixerim?

RHI. Genus et patriam tuam.[99]

CL. Genus non scires quanquam dicerem. Peregrinus sum longus de vestris finibus, infelix et infortunatus homo, virtute quamvis ornatus satis.[100]

RHI. Tui me satis mores delectant. Sed est mihi virgo domi, cuius me cura remordet. Si iuras pudiciciam amatum ‹fore› domus meae, te mecum ducam. Non austerum me nec malum dices.

CL. Per supremi regis regna iuro,[101] tuae domi me fidelem fore. Verum me sin habebis bene, longe tuus fuero; si secus —

RHI. Quid?

CL. Officium perficiam citius.

RHI. Oh, iustum est satis. Eamus.

CL. I prae. Sequor.

RHI. Nescio quid hoc sit. Me satis delectat adulescens, mores, vita.[102] Unum timeo, ne nimis familiaris fiat Anapausis. Longum istud non erit, hercle. Locabo illam viro, et potero alia pompa vivere. Si bonus erit, quod eius aetatis natus fuat, cuius gnatus meus, Clerus meus, bonum fuerit homini. Qui vocare, fili?

CL. Penthon.[103]

RHI. Tu mecum saepius ridebis. Gaude, fili.[104]

CL. Quod possum, facio.

RHI. Eamus.

CL. Sequor.

---

[99] Plautus: *Persa* 596–598: Quo genere aut qua in patria nata sit aut quibus parentibus, / ne temere hanc te emisse dicas suasu atque impulsu meo, / volo te percontari. *Captivi* 299–300: Meam nobilitatem occultare et genus et divitias meas, / Hegio; nunc quando patriam et libertatem perdidi.

[100] Plautus: *Captivi* 997: Sed eccum incedit huc ornatus haud ex suis virtutibus. Terence: *Adelphoe* 176: Si possiderem, ornatus esses ex tuis virtutibus.

[101] Plautus: *Amphitryon* 831–832: Per supremi regis regnum iuro et matrem familias / Iunonem.

[102] Terence: *Adelphoe* 758: Hancine vitam! hoscin mores! hanc dementiam!

[103] From πένθος: mourning, lamentation, grief.

[104] Terence: *Adelphoe* 755–756: Ita uti decet / hilarum ac lubentem fac te gnati in nuptiis.

RHY. Well, young man, what's up? Are you settled at the inn for a while?

CL. And the innkeeper's safeguarding my travel funds.

RHY. Haven't you arranged for servants to do that?

CL. I couldn't find one on a par with my station.

RHY. You don't want to answer what I asked you. But come eat lunch with me, I'll buy.

CL. What did you want to know that I haven't told you?

RHY. Your family and country.

CL. You wouldn't know my family, whatever I said. I'm a traveler from far beyond your borders, not too happy and not too lucky, but a good enough person, dressed in as much virtue as you'd wish.

RHY. Your bearing pleases me well. Now, I have a young lady at home whose care vexes me. If you swear you'll preserve the reputation of my house, I'll marry you into my family. You won't say I'm a callous father or a bad man.

CL. By the realms of the supreme king, I swear to keep faith with your house. If you'll really have me, I'll be yours come what may. If not —

RHY. What?

CL. I'd like to wrap up the ceremony right now.

RHY. Fair enough. Let's go.

CL. Lead on. I'll follow.

RHY. [*aside:*] I don't know what it is. The young man, his bearing, his life please me enough. But one thing I fear, that he'll get too familiar with Anapausis. That won't take long, by Hercules. All right — I'll marry her to the man, and I can live with the other foofaraw. He's about the age of my son, my Clerus, and if he works out, things will go well for him. What's your name, young man?

CL. Penthon.

RHY. [Mr. Gloom, eh? An undertaker's name.][105] You'll laugh more often with me, son. Be happy.

CL. I do the possible.

RHY. Let's go.

CL. Coming.

---

[105] An interpolation to capture the etymological flavor of "Penthon."

Aristopistes servus, Evangelus adulescens,

et Lorarius [106]

AR.   Quid nunc accusem magis?[107] Fortunam, quae me suppilavit herilibus pecuniis? An me, qui sic sapiens eram arbitratu meo? Hera, hera, sin hos rumores accipies, quid mihi scribarum dices? Quas optabis mortes, exitia, cruces? Ubi natus tuus, si me roges?

Sed quid de meme faciam miser? Hunc fraudavi, decepi babilonem,[108] exulem feci patria.[109] Pecuniam pene consumpsimus. O fidem Aristopistis! At quaerendus erat herus, et propter fidem fraude usus sum.[110] Quis credat?

EV.   Magnanimus istic fuit profecto, qui patrem ubicunque terrarum quaesivit. Maiorem fortunam auribus non memini audivisse meis.

LO.   Ni fallor, me fefellit Aristopistes. Quod ubi convenero, oh!

---

[106] Gloss: ὁ εὐαγγέλος, -ου bonus nuncius [evangelos: bringer of good tidings]

[107] Plautus: *Bacchides* 678: Pol tu quam nunc med accuses magis, si magis rem noveris.

[108] *Babylo, -onis*: wealthy person, nabob. Terence uses this word once, at *Adelphoe* 915.

[109] Plautus: *Rudens* 35–36: Qui huc Athenis exul venit, hau malus; / neque is adeo propter malitiam patria caret.

[110] Plautus: *Asinaria* 560–561: Ne illa edepol pro merito tuo memorari multa possunt: / ubi fidentem fraudaveris.

[SCENE 11: CRETE]

Aristopistes the Slave, Young Evangelus,

and Lorarius

[*Aristopistes rushes on from stage left, taking short little steps because of the chains around his ankles. He looks back to see if he's pursued. He's not*]

AR. What's more to blame now? My so-called luck, which made off with the master's money? Or just myself, and the wisdom I thought I had? But oh, mistress mine, if you believe these rumors, what would you say to me with sworn statements in front of you? What deceasings, dooms, and tortures would you pick? And if you asked me right now where your son is?

[*Rattling his chains*]

But what could I do even for myself? I've swindled my master, I've deceived a bumpkin playboy and made him an exile from his own country. And the money's had it. Oh, the loyalty of Aristopistes! But my master had to go on his search, and I gave back deceit for trust. Who'd believe it?

EV. [*Enters right, unnoticed*] How dedicated can you get, looking for a father in country after country? What a fate, what a fortune. My ears never heard the like of it.

LO. [*Enters left. Doesn't see the other two, though they both see him*] If I'm not deceiving myself, Aristopistes has deceived me. And when I find him, oh!

AR.   Sed certum est emori potius quam dolis in‹n›itar amplius. Modo conveni-
      rem herum, non dubito quin eloquentia sua placaret virum et hic tertius
      esset in infelici collegio nostro. Sin aliter, faxo per me sciat brevi, quod est.
LO.   Manibus primo provolvar in capil‹l›os. Monstrum hominis!
EV.   Adulescens, una hora.
AR.   Quis est qui me vocat?[111]
EV.   Qua venit?
AR.   Auscultabo ex insidiis quid loquatur.
LO.   Unguibus effodiam oculos.[112]
EV.   Patrem pene convenit.
AR.   Ohe, tantum est. Deus sum, si verum divinat animus.
LO.   Auris ambos obtru‹n›cabo.
EV.   Quem minus vidisset.
LO.   Mancum statim, post illum claudem fecero.
AR.   Arrige aures, Aristopiste.[113]
LO.   Post sic dentiloquus ad terram ut feram bestiam dabo.[114]
EV.   Divitias, genus, parentis, cognatos, nobilitatem convenit.[115]
AR.   Accedam propius profecto atque compellabo virum.

---

[111] Plautus: *Mercator* 808: Quis est qui me vocat?

[112] Plautus: *Aulularia* 189: Cui ego iam linguam praecidam atque oculos effodiam domi; *Captivi* 464: Oculos effodiam libens. Terence: *Eunuchus* 648: Ut ego unguibus facile illi in oculos involem venefico.

[113] Terence: *Andria* 933: Pam. Arrige auris, Pamphile!

[114] *dentiloquus*, i.e., *dentilegus*. Plautus: *Captivi* 796–798: Nam meus est ballista pugnus, cubitus catapultast mihi, / umerus aries, tum genu quemque icero ad terram dabo, / dentilegos omnes mortales faciam, quemque effendero.

[115] Plautus: *Captivi* 299: Meam nobilitatem occultare et genus et divitias meas; 411–412: Ut redire liceat ad parentis denuo, / cum apud hunc confessus es et genus et divitias meas.

AR. I'd rather die than live any longer by trickery. If I could just link up with the master, there's not a doubt that silver tongue of his would calm this fellow down, and he'd join our unhappy little band as its third member. But I've got to get word to him fast about what's going on.

LO. First I'll tear his hair out with my hands, the little freak!

EV. [*to Lorarius*] Young man, a moment of your time.

AR. Who's calling me? [*Turns and sees Evangelus trying to speak to Lorarius*]

EV. [*assessing Lorarius*] Where does he come from?

AR. I'll do a little eavesdropping on what he says.

LO. [*oblivious of Evangelus*] I'll gouge out his eyes with my fingernails.

EV. He looks just like the father.

AR. Ha! The spitting image. I must be a god, if my spirit ferrets out the truth.

LO. I'll cut off both his ears.

EV. He'd be the less for that.

LO. I'll cripple him right off so he'll walk with a limp.

AR. Prick up your ears, Aristopistes.

LO. After that, I'll collect his teeth, then give him to the earth like a wild beast.

EV. [*still gauging Lorarius*] He fits in terms of wealth, family, parentage, bloodline, nobility — they all match.

AR. I'll go right up to him and confront the man.

[*Aristopistes stealthily crosses to Evangelus as Lorarius is delivering the next speech. By the end of the speech, they are talking*]

LO. Sed ubi comperiam hominem? Ad portum fui, ad forum, in tonstrinis, in
     gymnasiis, in latomiis, in macello, in cetario, in caupoenis, omnibus de-
     nique in tabernis, argentariis, limbariis.[116] Ubi non quaesivi? Modo non
     abierit, satis est. Conveniam hominem profecto. Ecquid bene valetis, tibiae
     meae? Valebitis in horam, immo et in diem continuam? Tantum de vobis
     confido.[117] Deprecor vos, oro, supplico, miserum ne me linquatis. Vester
     ego sum, hominem si convenietis.[118]

EV. Peregrinus et hic est adulescens profecto, sed Graecus, etsi latina loquatur.
     Nostra iam fortuna declinat. Non tibi tantum timeo. Profecto Lyros[119]
     est. Delyrat equidem . . .

---

[116] Lists from Plautus: *Amphitryon* 1011–1014: Nam omnis plateas perreptavi, gymnasia et myropolia;
/ apud emporium atque in macello, in palaestra atque in foro, / in medicinis, in tonstrinis, apud omnis
aedis sacras / sum defessus quaeritando. *Epidicus* 195–199: Per urbem totam hominem quaesiveris. . . .
/ Utinam conveniam domi / Periphanem, per omnem urbem quem sum defessus quaerere: / per medi-
cinas, per tostrinas, in gymnasio atque in foro, / per myropolia et lanienas circumque argentarias.

[117] Literally, "I'm trusting you that much."

[118] See Plautus, *Mercator* 932 where young Charinus addresses his feet.

[119] Perhaps this is an allusion to Lyrus, who died childless; son of Aphrodite and Anchises, brother
of Aeneas. (Apollodorus, *Bibliotheca* 3.12.2). If so, its purpose here is opaque.

LO.   But where will I find him? I've been to the port and the forum, through the barber shops, the gymnasiums, and the stonemasons, around to the marketplace, the fish-pond, and the inns, and then to all the taverns, moneychangers' stalls, and the tailor shops. Where haven't I looked? He didn't just vanish, that's for sure. I've *got* to find the man. Feet, will you survive this? Will you be strong enough to keep going for another hour, maybe even the whole day? I trust you, feet, I'm in your hands. Please, feet, please — don't fail me now. I'm yours if you find the man.

EV.   [*to Aristopistes, of Lorarius*] He's a young man, a traveler, but a Greek even though he's speaking Latin. Oh, but then our luck turns bad. I'm not all that worried about you. But he's a real Lyros. He's raving mad ...

(¹²⁰   LO. [*Spots Aristopistes at last*] You!

AR.   Ah!

[*Flees, but with small steps because of his ankle chains. Lorarius grabs the chains and upends him. Drags him by his chains to center stage*]

LO.   First I'll tear out all your fingernails.

AR.   [*Looking with horror at his nails*] Ah!

EV.   [*to Lorarius*] I beg your pardon, sir.

LO.   Then I'll fix that ugly nose, it's much too big.

AR.   [*Crossing his hands over his nose*] Aahh!

EV.   Sir? Excuse me, sir.

LO.   And of course thieving runs in families, everyone knows that.

[*Unsheathing his knife*]

So I'll make sure you don't pass *that* along.

AR.   [*Crossing his hands over his lap*] Aahhh!!

EV.   Sir —

LO.   [*to Evangelus at last*] What!

EV.   By any chance would your name be Clerus?

LO.   [*Brandishing the dagger pointedly at Evangelus*] By any chance are you a Belgian noble?

---

¹²⁰ A page is missing from the unique manuscript of the plays, St. John's College, Cambridge MS. 60. The dialogue within parentheses is by the translator.

EV. A what?

AR. Why are you looking for someone named Clerus?

EV. His father has reason to believe the boy came here to Crete, and he's hired me to find him and the house where he's staying.

AR. His father's name?

EV. Rhystes.

AR. [*hands over ears*] Aah!

LO. Stop that!

EV. You know this Clerus?

AR. Know him? I am his ever-loyal slave, sir. Faithful through thick and thin.

LO. Slave?

AR. Through plenty and want.

LO. Slave!

AR. Yes.

LO. And your noble Belgian father?

AR. A little white figment.

LO. A slave. Aren't you ashamed?

AR. Ashamed, sir? Never! My real father was flogged to death, sir, like his own father, and his father's father before him. We have our pride!

LO. I can make sure the tradition continues.

AR. Don't go to any trouble.

LO. A slave, eh? Stuck with the truth, eh?

AR. I'm so embarrassed.

EV. If you're Clerus's faithful slave, where is he? His father lives close by.

AR. [*thinking fast*] Where is he? Why, uh — the last time we were on Crete, he deposited a large sum with Chrysolus the banker. He'll go straight there to claim his funds.

LO. Is that the truth?

AR. Would I lie to you?

EV. I'm going straight to the banker's and meet Clerus. You wait here for us. He'll want his slave back.

AR. We'll be right here. [*to Lorarius*] Won't we?

LO. All right.

[*Evangelus exits*]

This better be on the up and up. I'm tired of being conned by you.

AR. They'll be back here before lunch, [*aside:*] I hope, and then we'll have it made.

         ... maxime. Abundabimus argento.

LO.   Ubi?

AR.   Statim illuc una deducemur.

LO.   Quid est faciundum?

AR.   Stemus, praestolemur adulescentem.

LO.　Just what do we get out of this, anyway?

AR.　[*improvising wildly*] Uh, uh — why, I'll be set free, of course. And you, uh — you ...

LO.　[*ever the skeptic*] Yes?

AR.　[*suddenly inspired*] They'll give you a huge parcel of farmland right here on Crete.

LO.　I'll hold my breath.

AR.　Believe me. When we get to his father's place everything's going to be)[121]

great. We'll be loaded with money.

LO.　When?

AR.　They'll take us there directly.

LO.　And for now?

AR.　We stay here and wait for Clerus.

---

[121] The manuscript text resumes.

Epiichis mulier, Elpis ancilla, Rhystes senex,
et Clerus adulescens

PI.   Elpis, mea Elpis, curre, tuumque statim herum accerse. Miseram me, infortunatam me, invenustam mulierem!

EL.   Quid tibi fuit?

PI.   Mortua est vel continuo moritura nata.

EL.   Quid herus isti faciet meus? Hera, mea hera, filiae morbum etiam nescis.

PI.   Ah, iam ad Acherontem ibit.

EL.   Possum illam ego quo pacto liberare, sin ad illam vado.

PI.   Quid facturan?

EL.   Morbum pro parte levabo.[122]

PI.   Igitur curre. Conscende gradus.

EL.   Et tu descende. Sola me nunc opus est, hera.

PI.   Fiat.

EL.   Vado.

PI.   Iam vir meus molestia levabitur tantis sumptibus. Hem, quid agam? Quo me vertam? Cui iacturam narrabo meam, mihi qui valeat auxiliarier?

EL.   Anapausis, Anapausis!

PI.   Accur⟨r⟩ite, vicinae, amicae, ancillae! Funesta facta est familia nostra.

---

[122] Plautus: *Miles Gloriosus* 1272: Levandum morbum mulieri video.

[SCENE 12: CRETE]

Epiichis the Woman, Elpis the Maid,

[Anapausis the Young Girl], Old Rhystes, and

Young Clerus

[*Epiichis and Anapausis on the inner above*]

PI.   Elpis. Elpis! Run, fetch your master here, right now. Wretched me, unfortunate me — the woman unlucky in love!

EL.   [*Enters main stage*] What's the matter?

PI.   My daughter's dying, she's at the very point of death.

EL.   What would my master make of this? Oh, but mistress, you don't even know your daughter's illness yet.

PI.   Ah, she's already got one foot in the grave.

EL.   If I go to her, I can get her foot back out.

PI.   What will you do?

EL.   I'll help relieve this distress of hers.

PI.   Then run. Climb those steps.

EL.   And you come down. We need to be alone now, Lady.

PI.   Done.

EL.   On my way. [*Exits into house*]

PI.   Pretty soon my husband won't be annoyed by big expenses any more. What should I do? Where should I turn? Who can I talk to for help?

EL.   [*Enters inner above*] Anapausis, Anapausis!

PI.   Run — neighbors, friends, servants! Our family's teetering on the verge of a funeral.

[*Epiichis exits the inner above*]

EL.　Anapausis, nuncium apporto tibi peregrini, quem tu tantopere expetis.

AN.　Peregrini? Meorum amorum? Oh oh!

EL.　Ita. Non abiit. Hic est. Videbis hominem. Ne dubita.

AN.　Hem, ubi? Vidistin?

EL.　Vidi.

PI.　Tu, Anancha, curre. Tuum herum advoca verbis meis.

AN.　Ubi? aut cum quo?

EL.　Cum tuo patre una.

AN.　Ah ah! quando?

EL.　Modo.

RHI.　Fac fidelis fuas, et non servum te, filium potius habebo.

CL.　Ero.

AN.　Vox ad aures dei mihi nunc advolavit. Hem, tene me. Rege debilitatem meam.

EL.　Hera, quiesce. Quid illud est?

AN.　Audivi.

EL.　Quem?

AN.　Deum dico. Detege illam fenestram.

　　Oh, ah! Adest exoptatus, expetitus, expectatus, speratus meus. Vocem satis novi. Non possum hic esse. Elpis, ad illum vado.

EL.　Vide quid agas.[123] Non Rhodii sunt homines nostri. Primum te si quis videt, impudicam censebit.

---

[123] A standard caution in Roman comedy. Plautus: *Epidicus* 161: Epidice, vide quid agas, ita res subito haec obiectast tibi. *Persa* 610: Ehodum huc, virgo. Vide sis quid agas. Terence: *Eunuchus* 224: Vide quid agas. 964–965: Vide, Parmeno, / quid agas. *Phormio* 346: Senex adest: vide quid agas.

EL.   Anapausis, I've got news of the traveler, the one you've been wanting to meet so much.

AN.   The traveler? My love? Oh!

EL.   Here's how it is. He hasn't gone, he's here. You'll see the man, no doubt about it.

AN.   Well, where? Have you seen him?

EL.   With my own eyes.

PI.   [*Enters main stage with slave*] You, Anancha, run. Tell my husband I need him.

[*Anancha & Epiichis exit separately*]

AN.   Where was he? Who was he with?

EL.   With your father himself.

AN.   Ah! When?

EL.   Just now.

RHY.   [*Enters with Clerus*] Swear you'll be loyal, and I won't treat you like a slave, but a son.

CL.   You got it. [*They start toward the house*]

AN.   The voice of a god flies up to my ears. Oh, hold me — help me, I'm fainting.

EL.   Oh, hush, girl. What are you talking about?

AN.   I heard.

EL.   Who?

AN.   I say a god. Open that window.

[*Rhystes and Clerus are at the front door*]

Oh, ah! He's here — my longed-for lover, my sought-for sweetheart, my expected expatriate, my waited-for wonder. I know that voice, all right. I can't just stand here. Elpis, I'm going to him.

EL.   Watch what you're doing. Our people aren't from Rhodes, you know. If anyone sees you for the first time and you're like this, they'll think you have no shame.

AN.   Quid ego vulgum curo?

EL.   Et adulescens in discrimen veniet.

AN.   Istud nollem, ⟨a⟩ecastor. Potius ego moriar quam amores mei propter me
       quid patiantur mali.

EL.   Hera, gaude. Ingreditur aedes. Quid si diverteret?

AN.   Viverem, quiescerem, aedepol.

EL.   Ingressi sunt. Nunc in talamum ingredere, ne pater praesentiscat. Non du-
       bito quin huc pater et ipse recta veniant, ut quid subiti morbi venerit,
       cognoscant.

AN.   Iam valeo donec istic maneat.

EL.   Manebit. Tu in strato quiesce. Ego ad illos propero, ut quid —

AN.   Vade. Pr⟨a⟩estolor hic te.

EL.   Modo redibo.

PI.   Hau heu! Qui valet nata?

EL.   Valebit. Ne dubita. Iam resipiscit.

PI.   Quid morbi fuit?

EL.   Necdum scivisti quid illam agitaret morbi?

PI.   Minime.

EL.   At ego scio.

PI.   Quid est?

EL.   Quod fert adulescentia.

PI.   Quin dic quid est!

EL.   Amat.

PI.   Amat? Hem, amat? Quem amat?

EL.   Hunc adulescentulum, quicum herus modo ingressus est.

PI.   An est vir intus?

EL.   Est, et hic una quem adulescentulum dixi.

PI.   Quis? Aut cuiatis? Nonquid de nostris?

EL.   Minime. Mirificas vestis vestit. Haud memini peregrinos hunc in morem
       vestitos. Vestis brevis, contexta manica, candidata circum circa, in humeris
       pauca, in extremo lata satis.

PI.   Iugulandus est probe. Exitium nostrae familiae! Rhistes, Rhistes!

EL.   Vide quid facias, hera. Vin mortuam natam? Et aliquid in hunc
       machinato. Incredibile dictu fuat apud alios. Nunc bis tantum vidit
       adulescentem.

AN.   What do I care about people?

EL.   Even the young man, arriving at this very moment?

AN.   By Castor, I wouldn't want that. I'd rather die than have the people I love go through pain because of me.

EL.   [*Rhystes and Clerus are exiting into the house*] Be happy, girl. He's coming into the house. But what if he changes his mind?

AN.   I'd live, I'd die, by Pollux.

EL.   They've come in. Now into your bedroom, so your father doesn't figure it out. I'm sure he and your father will come straight here, and they'll find out a sudden illness has come upon you.

AN.   I'm fine now as long as he stays here.

EL.   Oh, he'll stick around. You keep quiet under the covers. I'll hustle over so what's —

AN.   Go. I'll wait for you here.

EL.   Be right back. [*Exits inner above as Epiichis enters main stage*]

PI.   Oh, wretched! [*Elpis enters main stage from the house*] How's the girl?

EL.   She'll be all right, don't worry about that. She's coming to her senses right now.

PI.   What was the sickness?

EL.   Don't you know her illness yet?

PI.   Of course not.

EL.   But I do.

PI.   What is it?

EL.   What youth always suffers.

PI.   Well, tell me what it is!

EL.   She's in love.

PI.   In love? What, in love? But who?

EL.   That stripling the master brought in this very second.

PI.   My husband's in the house?

EL.   He is, along with the young man I talked about.

PI.   Who is he? What country is he from? Isn't he one of us?

EL.   Oh, no. And he wears the most amazing clothing. I don't ever remember travelers dressing like this. A short tunic, woven sleeve, white all around, narrow at the shoulders, rather wide at the end.

PI.   We're absolutely done for. The ruin of our family! Rhystes, Rhystes!

EL.   Watch what you're doing, Lady. Do you want a dead daughter? And there's something at work in all this. It's an incredible thing to say in front of the others, but it's only twice now she's seen the young man.

PI.   Quando primo vidit?

EL.   Nunc agitur triduum. Dignus est, quem quisque diligat. Moritur hic?
        Mortua est nata. Abest hinc? Et anima natae devolabit.

PI.   Quid faciam misera?[124]

EL.   Quod sit in rem tuam.

PI.   Quid das consilii?

EL.   Ego nihil quicquam de morbo dicerem filiae. Iuvenem convenirem sciscita-
        remque diligenter, quidnam hic rerum agat peregrinus. Ad idque studerem
        quod in longum apud nos esset; et ad id laborarem, ut illum filia satis vi-
        deret, modo non festinus sit.

PI.   Festinus? Quomodo?

EL.   Modo dico, ne hinc abiturus.

PI.   Faciam ex consilio tuo. Tu ad natam vade. Illam consolare.

EL.   Fecero.

---

[124] Typically in Roman comedy, the master asks the slave for directions — interesting in this instance is the fact that Frulovisi has reversed the expected gender of both.

PI.   When did she see him first?

EL.   Three days ago. [*Epiichis is aghast*] We each love the one who's right for us. [*Epiichis is unimpressed*] Is she dying here? Your daughter's withering away. Is she gone yet? Your daughter's soul will fly away.

PI.   What do I have to do?

EL.   What you *can* do.

PI.   What do you think?

EL.   Don't say anything to anyone about her illness. I'll meet with the young man and ask some pointed questions, what business this traveler has here. Then I'll figure out what's in the future for us; and then after that I'll fix it so your daughter gets enough of a look at him, provided he's not in a hurry.

PI.   In a hurry? Why?

EL.   I only mention it in case he's on the point of leaving.

PI.   I'll do it. Go to my baby. Get her spirits back up.

EL.   You got it.

Epiichis mulier et Rhistes senex [125]

PI.   Sic est, ut dico, mi vir.

RH.   At ego dico tibi, mea uxor:[126] non possum ego pati, populi quod rumor fiam. "En decus hominis! Sine liberis Rhistes, senex ditissimus, puellam locavit virginem lepidam viro peregrino." Vel avariciae vel dementiae notam incurrero. Crimen tuum nullum erit, mulier. Profer quod, ut autumas, verum est. Amat adulescentula. Quod tunc dicent? "Non sunt hae pudicae nuptiae." Mulier, nihil curas nisi quae sunt grata in praesentia. Quid si mihi superstes sies, fatua, et casu intestatus moriar? Et puellus et puera peribunt fame. Tibi nec liberis quicquam prospectas, misera.

PI.   Quid ego faciam? Sic vult. Sic habeat. Liberos ego potius vivos et mendicos quam orba videri volo.[127]

RH.   Audi. Dotem ego nullam dabo, quando tu tuopte modo nuptias facis.[128]

PI.   Te quaeso, anime mi. Dotem dato, tantam saltem quantam habuisti de me. Te quietum ilico red‹d›idero, promittamque non repetituram.

RH.   Vin sic?

PI.   Immo sic te rogo atque obsecro.

RH.   Fac quod tibi videtur.

---

[125] Gloss: ἡ ἐπιεικής mitis [epieikes: mild, gentle]. ὁ ῥύστης liberator [rhystes: deliverer, one who sets free].

[126] A reprise of *mi vir, mea uxor*. See scene 9.

[127] Plautus: *Captivi* 321–323: Decere videatur magis, / me saturum servire apud te sumptu et vestitu tuo / potius quam illi, ubi minime honestumst, mendicantem vivere.

[128] As Walter Forehand states, typically in Roman comedy, "a young man is in love but unable to pursue his affair happily, primarily because of his father, who will not pay the expenses or disapproves of the relationship." (*Terence*, 124) With respect to his stepdaughter, Rhystes *senex* seems to perform his traditional father's role here with brio, yet the moment's considerable comic irony rests on the fact that he has himself just patched a wedding together on a whim.

[SCENE 13: CRETE]

Epiichis the Woman and Old Rhystes

EP. It's just as I'm telling you, dear husband.

RHY. But I'm telling you, dear wife: I cannot allow myself to become the butt of everyone's gossip. "Well, the honor of the man! Rhystes with no children, that filthy rich old man, and he's marrying his lovely young stepdaughter to a foreigner." I'll get a reputation either for avarice or insanity. Your accusation will be nothing, woman. Show us, as you say, what the truth is. The young girl's in love. But what do they say then? "This is not an honorable wedding." Woman, you only care about today. What if you outlive me, foolish thing that you are, and I died without a will? The boy and girl would starve to death. And you wouldn't get anything you're expecting for yourself or the children, you wretch.

EP. What should I do? She wants it this way, let her have it this way. I'd rather the children be alive and beggars, than seem deprived of offspring.

RHY. Listen. I give no dowry when you patch a wedding together on a whim.

EP. Dear heart, I ask you. Give a dowry that's at least as much as you got from me. I'll stop upsetting you all the time, and I won't go back to my old ways after the wedding — I promise.

RHY. This is how you want it?

EP. Oh yes, this way — please? Pretty please?

RHY. Do whatever seems good to you.

Evangelus et Clerus adulescentes,
Rhystes senex, et Aristopistes servus

EV. Hoc illud est quod novas nuptias caelebrare.[129]

AR. Sic opinor. Mater huius, propria quae fuerat uxor, e medio sublata est. Nunc vero sunt, hercle, veri coniuges. Sed ubi conveniam herum?

EV. Apud aedes illas habitant. Viden tu senem, illic qui pergit in ultima platea?

AR. Quem?

EV. Ellum senem illum.

AR. Eamus, obsecro, ut quid factum de hero —

EV. Accelera.

AR. Sic facio.

EV. Rhistes, hic te conventum quaerit.

RH. Quis?

AR. Servus tuus.

RH. Quis servus meus?

AR. Ego.[130]

RHY. Dis quidem essem sententia mea, si te possiderem.

AR. Servus sum ego generi tui. Sic et tuus.

---

[129] Previté-Orton flags *caelebrare* with a (*sic*). To be sure, *celebrare* means to celebrate or solemnize, but Frulovisi may intend a play on words here: *caelebs* means single, unmarried. I have deleted the flag and let *caelebrare* stand. See also Plautus: *Casina* 798–799: Age tibicen, dum illam educunt huc novam nuptam foras, / suavi cantu concelebra omnem hanc plateam hymenaeo mi.

[130] Plautus: *Curculio* 303–304: Pa. Te ille quaerit. Ph. Quid si adeamus? Heus Curculio, te volo. / Cu. Quis vocat? Quis nominat me? Ph. Qui te conventum cupit.

[SCENE 14: CRETE]

Evangelus and Clerus, Young Men,

Old Rhystes, and Aristopistes the Slave

EV.   This is where the coming wedding will be celebrated.

AR.   [*still chained*] So I think. His mother, who was a model wife, has been taken from our midst. But by Hercules, this is a proper match for sure. Where will I find my master, Clerus?

EV.   They live in that house. [*Sees Rhystes off left*] See that old man there who's coming down the last street?

AR.   Where?

EV.   That old man there.

AR.   Please, let's get going, so the master's arrangements —

EV.   Hurry.

AR.   That's what I'm doing.

EV.   Rhistes, here's a man who wants to meet you.

RHY. Who?

AR.   Your slave.

RHY. Who's my slave?

AR.   I am. [*Rattles his chains*]

RHY. It seems to me I'd be rich indeed, if I were your master.

AR.   I'm the slave of one of your family, so I'm yours, too.

RHY.   Ubi illum aut cum quo?

AR.   Captus immo relictus sum. Sed quid bene valet Clerus, herus meus?

RHY.   An est huic nomen Clero?

AR.   Sic est.

RHY.   Hoc est quod ex illo nunquam exculpere quivi. Cuiatis est hic herus tuus?

AR.   Graecus fuit huius pater. Patriam certam nescimus tamen. Mater Britan-
       ‹n›ica. Hic in Britan‹n›ia natus.

RHY.   Matris nomen?

AR.   Erichia.

RHY.   Quid illa? Vivitne?

AR.   Tantum nescio, sed per quietem illam mortuam saepius video: quod ve-
       rum esse coniecto. Nam quum adulescens se pararet ad iter, se mater con-
       ficiebat in lacrimas mortemque sibimet minabatur. Quid post sit actum,
       incertus sum penitus.

RHY.   Certe hic est gnatus meus.

AR.   Nomen tuum dic quod est.

RHY.   Quin tu dicito potius!

AR.   Graecum est non mihi notum nimis. Praeterea raro huiuscemodi nomen
       audivi.

RHY.   R‹h›istes sum.

AR.   Is es. Sed ubi conveniam Clerum?

RHY.   Transi mecum, sodes. Statim faxo hominem convenias.

AR.   Eo.

RHY.   Ingrediamur. Heus nobiscum, Evangele.

EV.   Libens fecero. Nam nihil est quod magis desiderem quam hunc finem bo-
       num videre.

RHY. [*Sees Aristopistes' chains*] When did this happen? Who did it?

AR. I was seized and yes, kept in chains. But does all go well with my master, Clerus?

RHY. Is that his name? Clerus?

AR. It is.

RHY. This is something I can't possibly forgive in him. What country is this master of yours from?

AR. His father was Greek. Even so, I don't know his exact homeland. His mother was British, and he was born in England.

RHY. [*alerting*] His mother's name?

AR. Erichia.

RHY. What, her? Does she live?

AR. That much I don't know, but very often I see her in that mortal stillness, and I believe it's true. For when the boy was getting ready for his journey, his mother was drowning herself with tears, and her own death was looming. But what happened after that, I really don't know.

RHY. This is my son for sure.

AR. Tell us what your name is.

RHY. Better you should speak!

AR. I'm not up on Greek, but I've rarely heard a name like that.

RHY. I'm Rhystes.

AR. You *are* he. But where am I to meet Clerus?

RHY. Why don't you come with me? I'll make sure you meet him right away.

AR. Willingly.

RHY. Let's go in. And Evangelus, come with us.

EV. I'd love to. There's nothing I'd rather do than watch this happy ending.

Clerus, Epiichis, Aristopistes,

Rhistes, et Evangelus

CL.   Tantum mihi pollicebar, mater: quod qui honeste viveret, perire non posset. Viden? Fortuna humana nos regit: artat ut lubet.[131] Modo divitem, modo mendicum me. Ego, cui servire solebant alii, in alterius servicium veneram,[132] et id faustum arbitrabar. Dei sunt qui nostros omnis humanos actus respiciunt.[133] Pro voluntate mea iusta me tandem respexerunt. En tibi gener et filius factus sum!

RH.   Fili, quid mihi nomen negabas et genus tuum?

CL.   Dicam, pater. Te minus noveram. Spes inerat tamen conveniundi patris, quod ubi foret actum, nolebam dici potuisset: "Et hic pro servo fuit."

RH.   Superbe factum.

PI.   Mi vir, et ego tot annos per te sic falsa fui.

RHY.   Non sunt haec in nuptiis memoranda tuis.

AR.   Verum est. Porro si non huic nupta fores, nec tam felices natae nuptias haberes.

CL.   Verum est. Cedant ista. Quid factum est, Aristopiste, de tuo Lorario?

AR.   Nescio. Verum de dimis mihi ablatus est, et, ut arbitror, in nervo datus.

---

[131] Thus Frulovisi recapitulates the play's theme of fortune. Plautus: *Captivi* 304: Sed viden? Fortuna humana fingit artatque ut lubet. *Truculentus* 217–219: Quod habebat nos habemus, / iste id habet quod nos habuimus. Humanum facinus factumst. / Actutum fortunae solent mutari, varia vitast.

[132] Frulovisi alludes to *Venus* and *servicium* in one last play on words. In addition, see Plautus: *Captivi* 306: Qui imperare insueram, nunc alterius imperio obsequor.

[133] Plautus: *Rudens* 1316: Di homines respiciunt: bene ego hinc praedatus ibo. Terence: *Andria* 642: Nisi quid di respiciunt, perdidi. *Phormio* 817: Di nos respiciunt: gnatam inveni nuptam cum tuo filio.

Clerus, Epiichis, Aristopistes,

Rhystes, and Evangelus

CL.   I've figured out this much, Mother: live honestly and you can't be a loser. You see? Human fortune rules us: it squeezes us to favor us. First I had money, then I was in want. I was used to having others serve me, then I came into a very different service and I thought that was lucky. The gods are the ones who care for us down to the last detail. Because I wanted to do what's right, they've cared for me through all of this. And look — I'm becoming your son-in-law and your son!

RHY.   But son, why did you deny your name and family to me?

CL.   I'll tell you, Father. I didn't know you all that well. Whatever else, hope depended on meeting my father, and whenever that happened, I didn't want anybody able to say, "He's been here looking like a slave."

RHY.   Superbly done.

PI.   My husband, so many years you've been deceiving me.

RHY.   These things aren't discussed at a wedding.

AR.   That's true. But if you hadn't married this woman, then you wouldn't be having such a happy wedding for your daughter.

CL.   You're right. It all ends well. Aristopistes, what happened to your friend Lorarius?

AR.   I don't know. It all got very confusing for me, but I think he was sent to prison.

EV.   Sic est. Ego illum conprehendi iussi.

CL.   Quo pacto te habuit, tibi quum custos fuit?

AR.   Ac si fuissem illius germanus frater, patru‹e›lis, aut saltem amitinus.

CL.   Nos igitur est aequum, boni ut homini quicquam faciamus.

RH.   Ager est quem in suburbio locamus: demus huic qui fruatur.[134] Fidelis
        fuit Aristopisti nostro, qui nostris semper bene consuluit et liberis et
        genero.

PI.   Fiat quod velis.

CL.   Aristopisti vero?

AR.   Tuis ego sumptibus vivere volo.

CL.   Immo liber esto.[135]

AR.   Liber est qui non servit iniusto domino.[136]

CL.   Accede huc. Te emitto manu.[137]

AR.   At istud munus ingratum est. Vivendum erit laboribus meis. Ego vixissem
        tuis.

RH.   Et nostris vives. Dabimus argenti tibi tantum in manu quod honeste
        vives.[138]

AR.   Et ego fidelis ero.

CL.   Semper fuisti. Sed ubi est iste Lorarius?

EV.   Ego statim et convenero et adduxero.

CL.   Adducito. Pater, hinc eo ad Anapausim coniugem et sororem meam.

RH.   Et nos te sequemur. Tu, Aristopiste, praestolare istos hic ante hostium.
        Mox introduxeris.

AR.   Fecero.

EV.   Quanta fortuna tam subita obiecta est istis.[139] Et patrem iste, filium ille
        convenere. Geminae nuptiae factae: iste molestia, fraude est illa liberata.

---

[134] Terence: *Adelphoe* 949–950: Agellist hic sub urbe paulum quod locitas foras: / huic demus qui fruatur.

[135] Plautus: *Epidicus* 730: At ob rem liber esto. *Menaechmi* 1028–1029: Mes. Si tuom negas me esse, abire liberum. Men. Mea quidem hercle causa liber esto atque ito quo voles.

[136] Plautus: *Captivi* 307–308: Et quidem si, proinde ut ipse fui imperator familiae, / habeam dominum, non verear ne iniuste aut graviter mi imperet.

[137] Terence: *Adelphoe* 970: Syra, eho accede huc ad me: liber esto.

[138] See *Adelphoe* 980–983, where Demea provides seed money to the just-freed Syrus.

[139] Another recapitulation of the theme of fortune. Terence: *Phormio* 841–842: O Fortuna, o Fors Fortuna, quantis commoditatibus, / quam subito meo ero Antiphoni ope vostra hunc onerastis diem.

EV.   That's right. I swore out a warrant against him.

CL.   How did he treat you when he was your guard?

AR.   As if I were his blood brother on his father's side. Or at least a distant cousin.

CL.   It's right then that we do such a man a good turn.

RHY.   The field we're farming near the city: let's give it to him for the income. He's been loyal to our Aristopistes, who has always looked after our interests well, both for the children and for a son-in-law.

PI.   I agree.

CL.   And for Aristopistes?

AR.   I only wish to live in your pay.

CL.   Now indeed be free.

AR.   He is free who serves not an unjust master.

CL.   Agree to this. I free you.

AR.   Oh, but that's a thankless gift — I've always lived off your generosity, and now I'll have to work for a living.

RHY.   No, you'll live off our means. We'll put money enough within your reach so you can live honestly.

AR.   And I'll be loyal indeed.

CL.   As you've always been. But where is this Lorarius?

EV.   I'll get him at once and bring him here.

CL.   Do. And Father, I'm going now to Anapausis, my wife and my sister.

RHY.   And we'll follow you. Aristopistes, wait here in front of the house for Evangelus and Lorarius. Bring them in right away.

AR.   That I'll do.

EV.   How lucky these unexpected obstacles turn out to be for them! This one meets his father, that one his son. Then wedding happiness doubles, as this one breaks free from his troubles, that one from fraud.

AR.   Ne expectetis, dum veniant. Mihi negocium datum est. Vos valete et plaudite.[140]

Finis

PEREGRINATIONIS

sextae comoediae T. Livii de Frulovisiis

Ferrariensis.

---

[140] The call for applause at the end of Roman comedies is pervasive.

AR.   No need to wait out here while they're on the way. I'll take care of that. [*to the audience:*] Now farewell and applaud.

The end of

TRAVEL ABROAD

the sixth comedy of T. Livius of

the Ferrarese Frulovisi.

The Fulovisi cipher *Tito Livio*, used here as a colophon to the play, comes from the copy of the *De Republica* held by the Biblioteca Municipale at Reggio Emilia, in MS. Coll. Turri F. 92. In this work written in dialogue form, each of the three participants is identified by an abbreviation of his name immediately before his speeches. In a few places in the MS. the scribe's designation for Frulovisi has been erased and the cipher inserted in its stead. In addition, the cipher appears on a few pages within the ambit of scribal decorations. I believe these cipher insertions are in Frulovisi's own hand.

APPENDIX

PLAYS OF PLAUTUS AND TERENCE CITED
IN THE TRANSLATION

Numbers indicate footnotes.

Plautus

Longer known plays

Amphitryon: 29, 44, 48, 75, 95, 101, 116
Asinaria: 11, 18, 36, 39, 49, 72, 110
Aulularia: 86, 88, 112
Captivi: 46, 50, 51, 60, 66, 69, 99, 100, 112, 114, 115, 127, 131, 132, 136
Casina: 51, 55, 129
Cistellaria: 79, 93
Curculio: 130
Epidicus: 116, 123, 135

Newly discovered plays in the Orsini Codex

Bacchides: 15, 107
Menaechmi: 18, 36, 41, 61, 95, 135
Mercator: 81, 111, 118
Miles Gloriosus: 88, 92, 122
Mostellaria: 29, 95
Persa: 99, 123
Poenulus: 3, 29, 44, 51
Pseudolus: 49, 51, 75
Rudens: 51, 55, 76, 109, 133
Truculentus: 28, 131
Stichus and *Trinummus,* both from the Orsini Codex, seem absent from *Peregrinatio.*

Terence

Adelphoe: 8, 42, 45, 46, 55, 70, 85, 92, 98, 100, 102, 104, 108, 134, 137, 138
Andria: 3, 16, 17, 54, 89, 98, 113, 133
Eunuchus: 3, 10, 40, 83, 87, 90, 95, 112, 123
Heautontimoromenos: 3, 15, 27, 56, 91
Hecyra: 10, 80, 94
Phormio: 3, 6, 21, 33, 51, 123, 133, 139

BIBLIOGRAPHY

WORKS OF FRULOVISI

Manuscripts:

St. John's College, Cambridge: MS. 60
  Corallaria, Claudi Duo, Emporia, Symmachus, Oratoria, Peregrinatio, and *Eugenius*
Biblioteca Municipale Reggio Emilia: MS. Coll. Turri F. 92
  De Re Publica
Biblioteca Capitular y Columbina: MS. 7.2.23
  De Re Publica and *Humfroidos Panegyricos*
Corpus Christi College, Cambridge: MS. 285
  Vita Henrici Quinti
College of Arms: MS. 12
  Vita Henrici Quinti
British Museum: MS. Cotton Claudius E. iii
  Vita Henrici Quinti and *Encomium Episcopi Bathoniensis*

Publications and Theses:

Vita Henrici Quinti, ed. Thomas Hearne. Oxford, 1716.
Opera Hactenus Inedita T. Livii de Frulovisiis, ed. C. W. Previté-Orton. Cambridge: Typis Academicae, 1932. Contains the comedies, *De Re Publica,* and the *Encomium.*
St. John, Helen Louise. "A Critical Edition of the *Vita Henrici Quinti* of Tito Livio Frulovisi." Ph.D. diss., University of Toronto, 1982.
———. "The *Vita Henrici Quinti* of Tito Livio Frulovisi." Master's thesis, University of Notre Dame, 1974. Latin text and English translation.

OTHER WORKS

Adams, J. N. *The Latin Sexual Vocabulary.* Baltimore: Johns Hopkins University Press, 1982.
Baldwin, Charles S. *Renaissance Literary Theory and Practice.* New York: Columbia University Press, 1939.

Bertanza, Enrico, and Giuseppe dalla Santa. *Documenti per la storia della cultura in Venezia*. Venezia: Spese della Società, 1907.

Binns, James W. *Intellectual Culture in Elizabethan and Jacobean England*. Leeds: Francis Cairns Ltd., 1990.

Blackwell, C. W. T. "Humanism and Politics in English Royal Biography: The Use of Cicero, Plutarch and Sallust in the *Vita Henrici Quinti* (1438) by Titus Livius de Frulovisi and the *Vita Henrici Septimi* (1500–1503) by Bernard André." In *Acta Conventus Neo-Latini Sanctandreani*, ed. I. D. McFarlane, 431–40. MRTS 38. Binghamton, NY: MRTS, 1986.

Borsa, Mario. "Pier Candido Decembri e l'umanesimo in Lombardia." *Archivio storico lombardo*, ser. 2, 20 (1893): 56–69.

Burckhardt, Jacob. *The Civilization of the Renaissance in Italy*. New York: Harper Colophon Books, 1958.

Cox, Virginia. *The Renaissance Dialogue*. Vol. 2 of *Cambridge Studies in Renaissance Literature and Culture*. Cambridge: Cambridge University Press, 1992.

Craster, H. H. E. "Index to Duke Humphrey's Gifts to the Old Library of the University in 1439, 1441, and 1444." *Bodleian Quarterly Record* I (1914–1916): 131–35.

Ferrari, Vincenzo, ed. *Studi di storia di letteratura e d'arte in onore di N. Campanini*. Reggio Emilia: Cooperativa Fra Lavoranti Tipografi, 1921.

Forehand, Walter E. *Terence*. Boston: Twayne Publishers, 1985.

Gardenal, Gianna. "Lodovico Foscarini e la medicina." In *Umanesimo e Rinascimento a Firenze e Venezia*, 3.1: 251–63. Firenze: Leo S. Olschki, 1983.

Gransden, Antonia. *Historical Writing in England*, vol. 2, *c. 1307 to the Early Sixteenth Century*. Ithaca: Cornell University Press, 1985.

Greene, Thomas M. "Petrarch and the Humanist Hermeneutic." In *Italian Literature: Roots and Branches*, ed. Giose Rimanelli and Kenneth John Atchity, 201–24. New Haven: Yale University Press, 1976.

Grendler, Paul F. *Schooling in Renaissance Italy*. Baltimore: Johns Hopkins University Press, 1989.

Griffiths, Ralph A. *The Reign of King Henry VI*. Berkeley: University of California Press, 1981.

Haller, Johannes. *Piero da Monte*. Rome: W. Regensberg, 1941.

Holinshed, Raphael. *Chronicles*, ed. Henry Ellis. 6 vols. London: J. Johnson, 1807–8.

Ianziti, Gary. *Humanistic Historiography under the Sforzas*. Oxford: Clarendon Press, 1988.

IJsewijn, Jozef. *Companion to Neo-Latin Studies*. New York: North-Holland Publishing Co., 1977.

Jacob, E. F. *The Fifteenth Century: 1399–1485*. Vol. 6 of *The Oxford History of England*. Oxford: Clarendon Press, 1961.

King, Margaret L. *Venetian Humanism in an Age of Patrician Dominance.* Princeton: Princeton University Press, 1986.

Kingsford, Charles L. "The Early Biographies of Henry V." *English Historical Review* 25 (1910): 58–92.

Kristeller, Paul Oskar. *Eight Philosophers of the Italian Renaissance.* Stanford: Stanford University Press, 1969.

———. *Iter Italicum: Accedunt Alia Itinera,* vol. 4. London and New York: The Warburg Institute, E. J. Brill, 1989.

Lehnerdt, Maximilian. "Review: *Opera Hactenus Inedita.*" *Gnomon* 10 (1934): 157–62.

Levy, Fred J. *Tudor Historical Thought.* San Marino, CA: The Huntington Library, 1967.

Ludwig, Walther. "Titus Livius de' Frulovisi — Ein humanistischer Dramatiker der Renaissance." *Humanistica Louvaniensia* 22 (1973): 39–76.

Machiavelli, Niccolò. *The Prince.* New York: New American Library, 1952.

Marsh, David. *The Quattrocento Dialogue.* Cambridge, MA, and London: Harvard University Press, 1980.

McLaughlin, Martin L. *Literary Imitation in the Italian Renaissance.* Oxford: Clarendon Press, 1995.

Mehus, Lorenzo, ed. *Leonardi Bruni Arretini Epistolarum libri VIII ad fidem codd. mss. suppleti.* Florence: ex Typographia Bernardi Paperini, 1741.

Merisalo, Outi. "Remarks on the Latin of Tito Livio Frulovisi." In *Acta Conventus Neo-Latini Hafniensis,* ed. R. Schnur, 663–68. MRTS 120. Binghamton, NY: MRTS, 1994.

Negri Rosio, Angela Maria. "Contributi per lo studio del *De re publica* di Tito Livio dei Frulovisi." *Rivista semestrale della biblioteca "A. Panizzi," Reggio Emilia* 1 (1977): 129–57; 2 (1978): 117–51.

Newald, Richard. "Livio, Tito, de Frulovisiis, *Opera Hactenus Inedita.*" In *A Bibliography of the Survival of the Classics:* 2.257–58. London: The Warburg Institute, 1938.

Oman, C. *The History of England from the Accession of Richard II to the Death of Richard III (1377–1485).* Vol. 4 of *The Political History of England.* London: Longmans, Green and Co., 1906; repr., New York: Greenwood Press, 1969.

Padoan, Giorgio. "La commedia rinascimentale a Venezia: dalla sperimentazione umanistica alla commedia 'regolare'." In *Dal primo Quattrocento al concilio di Trento,* ed. Girolamo Arnaldi & Manlio Pastore Stocchi, 3.3: 378–84. Vicenza: Neri Pozzo, 1981.

Picotti, Giovanni Battista. *Ricerche umanistiche.* Studi di lettere, storia e filosofia, 24. Firenze: La Nuova Italia, 1955.

———. "Le lettere di Lodovico Foscarini." *L'ateneo veneto* 32.1 (1909): 21–50.

Pigman, George W., III. "Versions of Imitation in the Renaissance." *Renaissance Quarterly* 33 (1980): 1–32.

Previté-Orton, C. W. "The Earlier Career of Titus Livius Frulovisiis." *English Historical Review* 30 (1915): 74–77.

Reynolds, Leighton D., ed. *Texts and Transmission: A Survey of the Latin Classics.* Oxford: Clarendon Press, 1983.

Russell, D. A. "De Imitatione." In *Creative Imitation and Latin Literature*, ed. David West and Tony Woodman, 1–16. Cambridge: Cambridge University Press, 1979.

Rymer, Thomas. *Foedera.* 20 vols. London: A. & J. Churchhill, 1704–1735.

Sabbadini, Remigio. "Il codice orsiniano di Plauto." In *Storia e critica di testi Latini*, 2nd ed., 241–59. Padua: Antenore, 1971.

———. "Tito Livio Frulovisio, umanista del secolo XV." *Giornale storico della letteratura italiana* 103 (1934): 55–81.

———. *Vita di Guarino Veronese.* Genoa: Sordomuti, 1891; repr., Turin: Bottega d'Erasmo, 1964.

Sammut, Alfredo. *Unfredo duca di Gloucester e gli umanisti italiani.* Firenze: G. C. Sansoni, 1967.

Sandys, John. *A History of Classical Scholarship.* New York: Hafner Publishing Co., 1958.

Shakespeare, William. *The Life of Henry the Fift‹h›.* Notes and Introduction by Walter George Stone. London: N. Trübner, 1880.

Smith, Grady. "Books and the Development of English Humanism." *Fifteenth-Century Studies* 6 (1983): 227–51.

———. "'Languida Virtus Semper ad Extremum': Titus Livius Frulovisi in England, 1437–39." *Fifteenth-Century Studies* 24 (1994): 323–33.

Smith, Thomas. *Catalogus Librorum Manuscriptorum Bibliothecae Cottoniae*, 1696; repr., Cambridge: D. S. Brewer, 1984.

Stäuble, Antonio. *La commedia umanistica del Quattrocento.* Firenze: Nella Sede Dell'Istituto Palazzo Strozzi, 1968.

Ullman, B. L. "Manuscripts of Duke Humphrey of Gloucester." *English Historical Review* 52 (1937): 670–72.

Watts, John. *Henry VI and the Politics of Kingship.* Cambridge: Cambridge University Press, 1996.

Weiss, Roberto. "Humphrey, Duke of Gloucester, and Tito Livio Frulovisi." In *Fritz Saxl, 1890–1948: A Volume of Memorial Essays from his Friends in England*, ed. D. J. Gordon, 218–27. London: Thomas Nelson & Sons, 1957.

———. "New Light on Humanism in England in the Fifteenth Century." *Journal of the Warburg and Courtauld Institutes* 30 (1951): 21–33.

———. *The Spread of Italian Humanism.* London: Hutchinson & Co., Ltd., 1964.

Wolffe, Bertram. *Henry VI.* London: Eyre Methuen, 1981.

Wylie, J. H. "Decembri's Version of the *Vita Henrici Quinti* by Tito Livio." *English Historical Review* 14 (1900): 84–89.

INDEX TO THE INTRODUCTION